A Dozen Great Ways to Recruit Disabled People

Leading edge practice on inclusive and accessible recruitment and selection

Jane Hatton

Published by
Elite Publishing Academy
www.elitepublishingacademy.co.uk

First Edition published 2017

Printed and bound in Great Britain by
Elite Publishing Academy

A catalogue record for this book
is available from The British Library
ISBN
978-1-912713-57-8

Praise for "A Dozen Great Ways"

"This book, Jane's sequel to "A Dozen Brilliant Reasons to Employ Disabled People", lists and illustrates how to break down the barriers people with disabilities face in recruitment.

A must read for any recruiter and seeker of talent, this book should be the foundation of any organisation that takes disability inclusion and recruitment seriously."

Michael Vermeersch,
Digital Inclusion Lead, Microsoft

"At last! The follow up to A Dozen Brilliant Reasons to Employ Disabled People! This book will arm you with the tools to move best practice recruitment theory to best practice actions.

If you are working towards a more diverse (and therefore more valuable) workforce then this is a 'must have' guide for all HR and Talent acquisition teams."

Jacqui Dobson,
FT, D&I Partner

"For too long our industry has been standardising recruitment processes with the goal of creating efficiencies. Today, it is encouraging that many recognise the benefits of designing user centric experiences but how often do we consider designing our

recruitment processes to be fair and without barriers for all potential applicants?

A Dozen Great Ways to Recruit Disabled People is a timely and fantastic read that shares valuable insights into best practices throughout the recruitment process. To anyone that is involved in recruitment, I highly recommend reading (and applying!) these insights".

Simon Clements,
Talent & Transformation Lead, IBM

"*This should be THE recruitment bible for all recruiters – because recruiting inclusively is good for everybody not just disabled people.*"

Maria Grazia Zedda,
Named in Power 100 UK's Top Influential Disabled People

"Many organisations say they value diversity and that inclusion is a priority, but they often forget to include disabled people! Believe me, as a diversity and inclusion consultant and somebody with a disability, I have seen this time and time again. But the next question from organisations is -- if we were to recruit more disabled people how on earth do we do it? It's really not rocket science, which is why Jane's latest book is fantastic.

Jane's book is packed with very practical advice and things that you can easily implement in your organisation. Jane challenges things like the appropriateness of 'culture fit' when recruiting somebody in perpetuating homogeneity.

Through to different ways of recruiting and interviewing which may actually get you a better candidate in the long run (and not just candidates who are disabled). Jane's book also reminds us of some of the building blocks in creating for diverse workplaces like the need to consider different models of disability (social, medical or charity) and the business case of recruiting people from different backgrounds and with diverse skills.

If any of my clients ask me how they can recruit more disabled people into their business. Hang on, urm, actually, if they ask me how to improve recruitment for everybody and not just disabled people -- I will be sending them a copy of this book."

Toby Mildon
Diversity and Inclusion Architect and
author of "Inclusive Growth"

"Once again, Jane has managed to put together a book for managers and employers which is practical, helpful and realistic. Too often books about diversity (in all its guises) are full of frameworks and theories which bear very little relation to real life. Jane comes at the subject from a personal lived experience perspective and tells it like it is! I would recommend this book to anyone either working to improve policies for people with disabilities or managing a person with a disability."

Paul Deemer,
Head of Diversity and Inclusion, NHS Employers

By the same author:

A Dozen Brilliant Reasons to Employ Disabled People

This book is a wholly accessible and vital read for anyone who wants to either start on a journey towards Inclusion or think about taking an alternative route to the one they are on."

Paul Deemer, MCIPD MSc,
Head of Diversity and Inclusion, NHS Employers

"For too long, employing disabled people has been seen as a nice thing to do. Jane's book provides evidence that employing disabled people benefits the business, and is a bottom-line commercial decision. Essential reading for those who wish to understand or make the business case for inclusion."

Dr Nasser Siabi OBE, CEO, Microlink

Contents

"If disability is not on your board agenda, neither is diversity (nor is innovation, productivity, brand experience, talent, risk, reputation...)"

The Valuable 500

Introduction

Making assumptions is something I usually try to avoid. But I'm going to start by making two assumptions. The first is that if you are reading this book, you probably recognise that most recruitment processes are no longer fit for purpose. If, indeed, they ever were.

The second assumption I have made is that you recognise the value of recruiting a more diverse workforce, although we will briefly re-visit this later. Many employers understand the need to attract and employ a different and more diverse range of talent, and yet continue using the same recruitment methods. I'm not sure who it was that said that madness is doing the same things and expecting different results (Einstein, maybe?).

Using the same recruitments methods is likely to result in recruiting the same kind of people. If we want to recruit different people, we need to do things differently.

So far, so good.

Have you heard the story about the experiment with monkeys in a cage, and bananas up a ladder? Whenever a monkey tried to go up the ladder to get the bananas, scientists would hose them all down with icy water, which they (understandably) hated. Eventually they stopped trying.

After a while, the scientists stopped the hosing and swapped a monkey. The new monkey didn't know about the hose, so he tried heading up the ladder, but all the other monkeys dragged him off. They didn't want another hosing. The new monkey didn't understand why, but he soon learned to stay away from that ladder.

Then they swapped another monkey. He tried going up too, but again, there was a scrap to avoid the hosing. Even the previous new monkey joined in even though he'd never been hosed before.

Eventually all the monkeys had been swapped. They would still stop any newcomers trying to get the bananas, even though they didn't know why. None of them had ever been hosed.

I researched this story, and it turns out not to be true, which is good news for the monkeys. But it is believable, because we do have a tendency to carry on behaviours long after they cease being useful. And, unfortunately, in many ways this applies to recruitment too.

So, what makes me think I might be able to suggest better ways of recruiting? Well, I'm privileged to have a number of different insights into the world of disability and employment.

First of all, I am a disabled person. One of the 83% of disabled people that became that way as an adult. In my case, at the age of 44. I have a spinal condition which I won't bore you with, but suffice to say that after three spinal surgeries so far (two on my lower spine and one on my neck), I am left with chronic pain in my lower back and neck, and pins and needles and low muscle strength in my left hand. This can create issues regarding sitting, walking, dealing with either the effects of severe pain or the side effects of pain relief (or both), and doing some everyday tasks.

This lived experience is invaluable in understanding the reality of disability (as opposed to the fear of what we think it would be like). Whilst I'd very much like to be without the pain, my situation is far from tragic (see models of disability, later), and having made lots of changes, I lead a very fulfilling and happy, if sometimes frustrating life. In my case, a move from the Midlands to London has meant I live in an environment that very much works for me (for other disabled people, the reverse may be the case – it's all situational).

However valuable this lived experience is though, I only really understand how this particular condition has affected me as an individual. Others with different impairments face different barriers to me, and others with the same condition will experience it differently.

In addition to my own experience, I have learned most of what I know about in this space from other disabled people. Long before becoming disabled myself, I was an Inclusion Consultant (although in those days we still talked about 'equal opportunities'), promoting the value of diversity and inclusion to employers. Some of my work involved engaging with 'Disabled Employee Groups' within a number of, mostly public sector, organisations. They taught me a lot about the subtle, and not-so-subtle, barriers that can impact on their access to the world of work.

My previous career in child care had shown me how little I knew about diversity and inclusion, and I undertook a Post-Grad course where my management report was around gender, and then a Masters degree where my dissertation was around race.

In a diversity training business I started and ran between 2004 and 2011, after becoming disabled, I employed people from a diverse range of backgrounds, in terms of ethnicity, gender, sexual orientation and disability, and learned so much from them.

In 2011 I founded the social enterprise Evenbreak, which is at the centre of the recruitment of disabled people. Evenbreak helps disabled people looking for work find opportunities with employers who will value their skills through a specialist job board built to the highest possible level of accessibility.

We work with many thousands of disabled candidates, from whom I learn something new every day. We work with employers who are trying to become more inclusive and accessible, and from whom I also learn new ideas and see how they work in practice. And we only employ disabled people ourselves, and we learn from each other all the time.

In addition to knowledge gained from my own lived experience, and the experience of those I work alongside and with, I try to keep up to date with current thinking and research in this space, including commissioning our own research.

The combination of this gives me real and helpful insights into what does and doesn't work in terms of inclusion and access in recruitment. The book includes personal learning, learning from others and reading around the subject. It also includes case studies from organisations who are leading in this field. Like all of us, I am continually learning and refining my thinking.

So, why do we need yet another book about recruitment? Well, as we have already hinted at, most current recruitment processes are ineffective in a number of ways. Not only do they exclude, or disadvantage, many disabled people (and others from diverse backgrounds), they are also fairly poor at finding the best person for the job in general. How can we improve the recruitment experience for candidates (in being able to apply on an equal footing) and for employers (in finding the genuinely best person for the job)?

Frost and Kalman (2016)[1] suggest that, 'The very nature of recruitment can be biased towards conservative, seemingly more risk averse candidates.'

Recruitment is a risk averse activity, and rightly so. The impact – financially and otherwise – of hiring someone who turns out not to be suitable is substantial. However, Frost and Kalman go on to suggest that, 'Breaking the norm could be more accurately described as brave rather than risky. Hiring someone of a different gender, age group, nationality or ethnic background may stand out more but it doesn't necessarily mean it's more risky. People with the confidence to challenge the status quo may be more able to make necessary changes and challenge current thinking.'

Speed is often seen as an essential feature of recruitment. Often a major KPI (Key Performance Indicator) of the recruitment process is time to hire. Again, this is understandable. If a team is missing key roles, productivity can be affected. Line managers will want vacancies or newly-created roles to be filled very quickly. The outcome of taking a long time to hire can mean short-term problems for the company.

However, a quick process can create long-term problems for the company. Quick hires aren't necessarily the best hires, and they may well fail to meet the strategic needs of the organisation as a whole.

Recruitment – the whole talent acquisition piece – should be seen as strategic, rather than operational.

Frost and Kalman (2016)[1] state that, 'Taking a longer-term view, seeing the organisation as a whole and thinking of scale enables managers to fish in a larger talent pool, naturally opening up the opportunity to attract and select a more diverse range of people.'

They add, 'Inclusive talent management is concerned with enlarging the toolbox at an organisation's disposal and increasing the diversity of tools on offer to help solve the challenges the organisation faces. Instead of hiring more brilliant (but similar) people, we are actively looking for difference.'

Purpose of this book

This book can be used in a number of different ways. It may be that you just want to check that your recruitment processes are as inclusive as they can be, and make minor tweaks where they aren't.

It may be that parts of your recruitment process need a bit of a re-vamp to reduce some of the barriers they pose to candidates.

Or it may be that you realise your recruitment process needs a complete re-fresh. Starting again with a blank canvas.

You, or your organisation, might not be comfortable with some of the suggestions which stray too far from the comfortable and familiar. I've seen recruiters throw their hands up with horror at the very thought of using anything other than CVs and interviews to assess candidates!

Whether you are looking to make minor tweaks or radical changes to your current recruitment practices, this book can help you explore options. And the most important outcome is that whatever changes you make, your processes become more inclusive and accessible. And therefore, more effective for everyone.

What we find, of course, is that if changes are made to reduce barriers for disabled candidates, everyone benefits. All candidates (not just those with impairments) will be able

to demonstrate their abilities more effectively, and employers will be in a much better position to find the very best talent.

Without wishing to throw any spoilers in at this point (I don't want to pre-empt any 'Aha' moments from later on), we might find that CVs offer very few candidates an appropriate vehicle to demonstrate their suitability for a particular role.

There is much evidence about the unconscious (or conscious) impact a non-Western sounding name can have on a recruiter. Or a seemingly female name. Or which school a candidate went to. Or where they live. Yet none of these factors will bear any relation to the candidate's capacity to perform well in a given role.

The trope, so often trotted out, of "we treat every candidate the same" lost any credibility a long time ago. As we know, treating everyone the same is not the same as equality. Enabling everyone to compete on a level playing field means treating people according to their requirements.

Brown, J (2016)[2] reminds us that, 'Providing the same starting line for employees doesn't mean that everyone actually starts from the same place. It is essential to understand how employees get to the starting line in the first place – the hurdles they face in the career race that may be invisible to you – in order to create truly equal opportunities in the workplace.'

This is one of those areas where success breeds success.

Employing disabled people enables the organisation to see the benefits, and that it's all much easier than anticipated. The fear of the unknown reduces. And the more disabled people you employ, the more familiar and comfortable all your people are around disability. Your reputation as an inclusive employer of choice is enhanced, and more disabled people will apply. It's a virtuous circle. And the real winner is the business, who now has more of that previously-untapped talent.

It's important to note that people with invisible and/or fluctuating conditions are included too. These are people who are less likely to be open about their impairments unless they feel very safe to do so.

While the purpose of this book is to ensure recruitment processes are open, inclusive and accessible to disabled candidates, the inevitable outcomes will be recruitment practices that work much more effectively for everyone – all candidates, and all recruiters who are genuinely seeking talent.

Models of disability

Over time, 'disability' has been viewed in a number of ways, and various models have informed the thinking around it. All have their dangers, and all have something valuable to offer. These are my views on each.

The Charity Model

The most common model is the charity model. We picture the pretty little blonde girl in leg irons holding a charity tin and appealing to the rich for a few coppers. Or the adverts on TV, portraying the lives of disabled people as some sort of tragedy, which will tug on the heart strings and encourage people to donate money, either through guilt or compassion.

What could be wrong with compassion? Well, in order to effectively tug on those old heart strings, disabled people must be seen as objects of pity. Passive creatures, dependent on the generosity of others to have any quality of life. Incapable of independence, either in thought or in life. People whose existence is miserable. People whose lives no-one would want to live. Due to their primary purpose – fund-raising – charities have to dwell on the very worst aspects of being disabled. It divides us into those 'lucky' enough not to be disabled, and those 'unfortunate' enough to 'suffer with' some awful condition.

In reality, of course, nothing is that black and white. There is no 'us' and 'them'. Anyone can become disabled, through accident or acquiring a long-term health condition. In fact,

83% of disabled people weren't born with their impairment, so any charity donor could become disabled at any moment, if they aren't already.

And portraying disability as tragic is problematic in other ways, too. In terms of access to employment (which is essentially what this book is about), employers may think of disabled people as 'objects of pity' or 'charity cases'. They might have a collection for a local or national charity, or even have charity-giving as a core part of their Corporate Social Responsibility strategy. Many large corporates have a 'Charity of the Year' that employees can raise money for, or even volunteer within. But the thought of employing a disabled person, if it occurs at all, would be considered a charitable act. Giving this poor soul an opportunity. Doing them a favour.

This view certainly doesn't help employers to see disabled people as a valuable source of talent, or having skills that can improve an organisation.

The old charity model of putting disabled people away in institutions so they could be 'looked after' is thankfully less prevalent now. And some charities do some good work in terms of campaigning for the human rights of disabled people. There is a (far too slow) trend for disability charities to be run by, or at least informed by, people with lived experience of disability. But in the main, the charity model is still seen as dividing people into the givers and receivers of charity.

And even the good work that some charities do should

really be delivered by the state as a right, as opposed to services that rely on the charitable, and therefore, discretionary, donations of other people.

Whatever your politics, seeing disabled people as objects of pity or charity cases, is unlikely to help us be seen as fantastic potential recruits in the business world.

The Medical Model

This is also known as the Deficit Model, or the Individual Model. It says people are disabled by their impairments or differences.

Under the medical model, these impairments or differences are seen as medical problems which should be 'fixed' or changed by medical and other treatments, even when the impairment or difference does not cause pain or illness.

The medical model looks at what is 'wrong' with the person and not what the person needs. It can create low expectations or lead to people losing independence, choice and control in their own lives.

The model is based on what an ideal or 'normal' person is perceived to be like, and in what ways the disabled person deviates from this – hence the deficit. The goal, therefore, is to make everyone as 'normal' as possible, using the assumption that difference is intrinsically a bad thing, to be avoided if at all possible.

There are some benefits to looking at the medical aspects of impairment. Where symptoms of a condition involve pain, or other unpleasant feelings, then many people will welcome medical intervention to alleviate them. Speaking personally, I very much welcome any medical advances in finding effective pain relief which involves no, or few, side effects. I am pleased that doctors, chemists and pharmacists are using science to improve lives.

However, as a society, the medical model can be dangerous. It offers the view that we should all conform to some arbitrary idea of what a 'normal' person is. The problem is therefore seen to revolve around the way in which a person differs from this – the ways in which they are 'abnormal', or what is 'wrong' with them. The problem is the individual, and it's up to the medical profession to solve the problem. It also promotes discriminating against disabled people (who wants to employ people who need to be 'fixed'?).

This, of course, has a number of questions. Who decides what 'normal' is? What about people who can't be 'fixed'? What relevance is any of this to people who are neither disabled nor in the medical profession? Is it really the case that society is best when made up of people who are all the same?

The Social Model

The social model originates from the disability rights movement. In 1975, the UK organisation Union of the

Physically Impaired Against Segregation (UPIAS) claimed, 'In our view it is society which disables physically impaired people. Disability is something imposed on top of our impairments by the way we are unnecessarily isolated and excluded from full participation in society.'

This model removes the focus of the problem from the person and their differences, and locates it within society. People are disabled not by their impairments, but by the barriers that society puts in the way. It is less about impairment, and more about access. It highlights the importance of removing social, environmental, structural, attitudinal, technological and physical barriers to the inclusion and participation of disabled people.

This has been a huge breakthrough. To give an obvious example, a wheelchair-user is not disabled by the need to use a wheelchair, but by the stairs, narrow door-ways or cobbled streets that are in their way. In a world where level access, wide doorways and lifts were the norm, wheelchair users would be far less disabled. Similarly, if everyone were taught sign language growing up, Deaf people would be far less disabled.

To use myself as an example, living in a suburb in the Midlands with little public transport, I spent most of my time isolated at home. Finding sitting very painful, I would work from my bed; my laptop on a table above me. Being unable to drive for more than a few minutes (because of the sitting), most meetings would require me to be driven by a driver paid for by Access to Work, with me lying down in the car.

This meant that every meeting (especially those in London, which was a large proportion of them) had to be planned like a military exercise. A seven-hour (or more) round trip, causing huge pain spikes which took days to recover from. Or an overnight stay – which either meant my driver doing two journeys, or considering an overnight stay for both of us, and the even more expensive question of where to park a car overnight in London. So, I limited my meetings to absolute essentials, meaning I was absent from many events.

I felt like an invalid (literally – not valid), dependent on others to participate, or not participating at all.

On moving to London, I am able to use public transport to travel around the city (standing on buses or tubes) independently and spontaneously. I can attend meetings, events and conferences (standing throughout), and have a great and varied social life. I have the same impairment, but am so much less disabled because of the environment around me.

When we base our practice on the social model, we focus on reducing or removing disabling barriers. It's not about fixing people, it's about creating a world where disabling barriers no longer prevent people from achieving their goals, aspirations and full potential. It recognises disabled people as full, valued and included members of our communities with the same rights and responsibilities as everyone else.

Of course, life is never quite as simple as that, and the social model has its drawbacks too. However society arranges itself, I will still have chronic pain and muscle weakness. A blind person will still have sight loss and so on.

In recruitment, the important thing is to identify barriers that might disable candidates from applying, and might prevent them from being assessed in ways which demonstrate their talents, putting them at a huge disadvantage when compared with non-disabled candidates. In this book, we will look at the barriers which might be present at each part of the recruitment process, and suggest ways of removing them, or at least reducing their impact.

As an aside, in the UK we use the term 'disabled people' to refer to the fact that we are disabled by our environment. In other countries the people-first term 'people with disabilities' or even 'persons with disabilities' is preferred. As I am UK-based and very much subscribe to the social model, the term 'disabled people' will be used throughout the book.

Whilst none of the models are ideal, the social model is the most useful in terms of what we can do within organisations to ensure we don't exclude those who may well be the best candidates.

The problem isn't the disabled person, it's the disabling barriers we face. And, as we shall see, *they* can and should be fixed.

A reminder of the business case

We know that the narrative that we hold about disabled people will strongly influence our actions and behaviours. If we see disabled people as objects of pity who need a hand-out, our processes and decision-making will reflect this. And if we see disabled candidates as presenting us with problems, this is bound to impact on our decision about whether or not to hire them.

It's only when employers see disabled candidates as a valuable source of talent that everything else falls into place.

We examined the business case for employing disabled people in the previous book, A Dozen Brilliant Reasons to Employ Disabled People[3], and so will just offer a brief reminder here.

1. Including disabled people in your search for talent increases your chances of attracting the right person for the job. Around 20% of people of working age are disabled or have a long-term health condition. Excluding this large group of people means you are missing out on a large pool of talent

2. On average disabled people are just as productive as non-disabled people - sometimes more so (consider someone using speech-to-text software, who may be quicker and more accurate than their non-disabled counterpart)

3. On average disabled people have significantly less time off sick than our non-disabled colleagues – sometimes up to 30% less

4. Disabled people tend to stay in our jobs longer, increasing retention. This can save huge amounts of money in recruitment, training and managing with unfilled positions

5. Disabled people have, on average, fewer workplace accidents. People who are more vulnerable to accidents take extra care to ensure our own, and others' safety

6. Disabled people and our families are consumers with valuable spending power. Up to £250 billion a year in the UK alone. Employing disabled people gives you valuable internal intelligence on how to attract this market

7. Disabled people often develop skills in innovation and creativity to navigate round a world not designed for us. Creative problem-solving. Resilience. Innovation. Determination. Useful skills for your business!

8. Disabled people may have additional skills which your organisation would benefit from, including different and valuable ways of thinking, challenging the spectre of 'group think' and complacency

9. Having a good reputation for inclusion attracts more customers and the best candidates – disabled or otherwise. Many candidates look for evidence of positive

social and environmental impact in prospective employers

10. Being a good inclusive employer raises morale amongst all your employees. 2% of people of working age acquire a disability or long-term health condition every year. If they see that you value staff this happens to, they will feel more valued

11. Incorporating best inclusive employment practices within your own organisation makes Corporate Social Responsibility real. It's not just about raising money for charity, it's about being an ethical organisation in all its practices

12. There is widespread proof of the business benefits of a diverse workforce. Disability forms an important part of that (although it is often ignored)

13. The benefits of inclusion go far beyond helping disabled people - everyone benefits. An open, diverse, flexible, ethical and inclusive culture provides a better workplace for all employees. People with hidden/invisible impairments are less likely to feel they should 'mask' themselves at work, and will be far more productive if they can be their true selves.

14. The costs associated with inclusion are far less than you think, and the benefits far outweigh them

Since then, new research from Accenture in 2018[4], in

partnership with Disability:IN and the American Association of People with Disabilities (AAPD), reveals that companies that embrace best practices for employing and supporting more disabled people in their workforce have outperformed their peers. The research showed that, 'Leading companies that are working successfully toward disability inclusion have also achieved tangible financial benefits. For example, the research shows that leading companies were, on average, twice as likely to have higher total shareholder returns than those of their peer group.'

They also reported that, 'Champions [those that stood out for leadership in areas specific to disability employment and inclusion] achieved – on average – 28 percent higher revenue, double the net income and 30 percent higher economic profit margins over the four-year period we analysed.'

A Boston Consulting Group study of more than 1,700 companies around the world[5] shows that diversity increases the capacity for innovation by expanding the range of a company's ideas and options, leading to better financial performance.

So, we know that employing disabled people absolutely makes fundamental business sense, as well as all the other good reasons to do so. And yet, the gap between the proportion of disabled people in work compared with non-disabled people is still huge (remaining stubbornly at around 30%). Understanding the business case is a great start, but on its own, is clearly not enough unless and until we change our processes, practices and behaviour.

Using third parties

Many organisations outsource all or part of the recruitment process to third parties. There may be many good operational or financial reasons for doing this.

However, Sweeney & Bothwick (2016)[6] warn that 'Agencies might be OK for high-volume recruiting, but be mindful of the diversity of the candidates they are putting forward as well as the employer brand they are portraying of your company in the market.'

The responsibility for accessing a diverse workforce, and offering an inclusive and accessible recruitment process lies with the employer. The best agencies are pro-active at suggesting ways of attracting diverse candidates, and knowing how to remove barriers from the recruitment process, but sadly these agencies are few and far between.

The first sift by an agency might exclude the very candidates you want. Most disabled candidates won't mention their access needs to a recruitment agency, so the agency might unwittingly discriminate against them due to gaps in their CV.

Make sure agency completely understand your genuine commitment to wanting to actively attract diverse candidates, and that you expect to receive a diverse range of candidates from them.

Sweeney & Bothwick[6] offer the following tips around using

third party providers:

- ‘Make sure they are aware of your commitment to receiving diverse candidate lists. Discuss with them where they will source their candidates from and how

- Consider using at least one organisation that specialises in resourcing diverse candidates

- Make sure they are up to speed with your focus on D & I and can talk to candidates about your progress’

It’s important, of course, to monitor the diversity of candidates you receive from an agency. If they don’t share your commitment, and don’t provide you with a diverse range of suitable candidates, you will need to manage that relationship, or change provider.

Some organisations use specialist job boards directly, using their in-house team, alongside their agency.

Measuring Success

The most obvious way to measure the success of your recruitment process is to monitor the number of disabled people who are successful in gaining employment with you. It's also important to monitor retention and career progression rates of course, but we are focusing on recruitment here.

Monitoring for disability can be difficult, because most (around 80%) of disabled people have 'hidden' or 'invisible' conditions. Whilst someone using a wheelchair, or a guide dog, or someone with Down's Syndrome may have outward signs of their impairment, someone with autism, diabetes, schizophrenia or hearing loss may not.

We know that (often for very good reasons) a high proportion of disabled people will hide or mask their condition at work. This isn't a reason not to monitor for disability. But in order to monitor effectively, disabled candidates and employees need to feel safe to be open about their condition – at least on confidential monitoring forms.

Whilst striving to create this open, trusting and 'safe' culture, monitoring is still useful. The initial aim will be to reduce the number of people ticking 'prefer not to say'. This measures the degree to which people feel able to be honest, and can be a useful measure of the degree to which the culture is genuinely felt to be inclusive.

If we aim to have a more diverse workforce, we will have no idea if we are achieving it in terms of disability unless we measure it. If a group is particularly under-represented, this may indicate that barriers are present, which need to be investigated. And measuring it is a clear message that it's something we value.

Monitoring is only part of the process; the data gained needs to be put to good use.

Frost and Kalman (2016)[1] state that, 'Integrating diversity data in management information is akin to integrating the strategic workforce plan in annual business planning. It can add significant value as it provokes profound questions, at the right moments, about how an organisation manages its talent.'

It's important that diversity and inclusion aims, targets and measurements are central to business strategy rather than being seen as something somehow separate and 'bolted on'. Frost and Kalman[1] go on to say, 'People behave very differently when their decisions are transparent. People expect to be held accountable for profit and loss, so if we value diversity why not hold them to the same standard and make them accountable for the diversity of their recruitment?'

In recruitment, however, the diversity of the candidates and successful recruits isn't the only measure of success. In fact, in woefully few organisations it isn't measured at all.

A very common measurement in recruitment is time to hire. Often recruiters have 'time to hire' as their primary Key Performance Indicator. The quicker they hire someone, the faster they get paid and the better the ratio of effort and reward. Frost and Kalman compare it to an airline that only gets paid when its planes are in the air as opposed to being on the ground, the incentive is to speed up the turnaround time. This causes problems when it comes to diversity.

As we have seen, speed of hire is rarely related to quality of hire, and a long-term strategic view will be more concerned about the suitability of the person, their adaptability, and the contribution they can make to the organisation as a whole rather than saving a week on the hiring process.

Forward planning can often save more time in the hiring process than cutting corners.

Back to encouraging candidates to be open about their impairment and/or access needs. How do we help disabled candidates feel safe to be open?

Interesting research by von Schrader et al (2016)[7] found that the most important factors (those felt to be 'very important') which encouraged disabled candidates to be open about their impairment were:

- Need for accommodation 68.2%
- Supportive supervisor relationship 63.5%
- Disability friendly workplace 56.8%
- Active disability recruiting 50.5%

- Knowing of other successes 49.9%
- Disability in diversity statement 48.9%
- Belief in new opportunities 40.7%

Not surprisingly, their research showed that 'very important' factors when deciding not to mention their disability were:

- Risk of being fired/not hired 73.0%
- Employer may focus on disability 62.0%
- Risk of losing health care 61.5%
- Fear of limited opportunities 61.1%
- Supervisor may not be supportive 60.1%
- Risk being treated differently 57.8%
- Risk being viewed differently 53.8%
- No impact on job ability 44.0%
- Desire for privacy 27.9%

So, it's important to reassure candidates that being open from the start will help you to provide any support they might need, and that it won't disadvantage them in any way.

Inclusion and Intersectionality

Many employers seem to put people into separate boxes and deal with them separately. "We're focusing on the gender pay gap this year" or "Attracting BAME candidates is our priority at the moment". A Black woman might wonder which box she fits into for this organisation. And is a Black gay person included in the BAME initiative, or do they have to wait for LGBTQ+ to have their turn?

And what happens when the new initiative is introduced? Do we then abandon last year's 'type' of people and move on to the next group?

The reality is that inclusion is inclusion. Being 'a bit' inclusive is not possible – it's like being 'a bit' pregnant. If you are focusing on gender, but not, say, LGBTQ+, that's not inclusion.

The good news is that most practices around improving inclusion benefit everyone. Flexible working, perhaps initially introduced to help women returners, benefits many other employees too. Men with young families. People with other caring responsibilities. Someone who hates travelling in the rush hour. A person whose health condition or disability prevents them working full time.

An accessible building, with lifts and automatic doors, makes it easier for everyone to get around. Employees carrying equipment, for example.
So instead of putting people into boxes, accept that most

people don't conveniently sit (or in my case, stand) in one box. We all have differences which overlap, intersect and sometimes change over time. Inclusion means focusing on removing barriers for everyone, not just a select few.

At Evenbreak, whilst only employing people with lived experience of disability, we have an amazingly diverse team in other ways too. Ethnicity, gender, age, sexual orientation, family circumstances, location, the lot! And we include a range of impairments including neurodiversity, mental health, visual impairment, hearing impairment, physical impairment and chronic pain, both acquired and from birth.

Whilst our focus is disability, we are very aware that disability itself doesn't discriminate. Anyone, from any background, can be born with, or acquire a long-term health condition or impairment. Our candidates are wonderfully diverse. In some recent research carried out by Applied[8], Evenbreak appeared in the top 10 job boards for ethnicity and gender, although those aren't our 'target' audience.

There will be specific actions that will help particular groups more than others, and positive action for under-represented groups is very much to be encouraged. Just saying 'we welcome everyone' won't address the factors which discriminate, perhaps unwittingly, against many people. The aim is to anticipate and address barriers faced by anyone, especially through involving those people in decisions.

"Culture eats strategy for breakfast."

Peter Drucker

Part One

Start at the Beginning

Great Way #1: Create an Inclusive Culture

An important point to note is that although I positioned this first in the sequence of chapters, it is not the case that your culture has to be perfectly inclusive before you start to think about hiring disabled people. Many recruiters tell me they don't want to start attracting disabled candidates until 'everything is in place' (I've yet to find an organisation – including my own – where *everything* is in place!).

Firstly, whether or not you are aware of it, you will almost certainly already be employing disabled people. Most impairments – around 80% - are not visible, and, as we've already discovered, many disabled people don't mention their disability to their employer. Also, many people don't identify as a 'disabled person' even though the definition of disability in the Equality Act 2010 would include them.

Secondly, and most importantly, the best way to ensure your organisational culture becomes more welcoming to any particular group of people is to include them in that process.

The more disabled people that are active in each part of the organisation, and the more they become a familiar sight, the more the ignorance and fear of those around them (the greatest barriers to an inclusive culture) are reduced.

Otherwise, you will be trying to second guess what disabled people might need without actually involving them in that discussion.

That's not to say that you shouldn't be anticipatory, and remove the barriers you know about. But the less obvious barriers (sometimes structural, but more often around processes, attitudes and behaviours) can be more easily identified, and remedies suggested, by those who are impacted by those barriers.

Changing your culture to become more inclusive requires the same project management and change management techniques that you would use to introduce any change, such as a new IT system, or a re-structure.

Sweeney & Bothwick (2016)[6] suggest that, 'Many D & I [Diversity and Inclusion] programmes, although positioned as attempting to change the culture and structures within organisations, actually have no change management principles wrapped around them. The majority of these programmes are focused on initiatives, a number of separate actions and deliverables pulled together on a spreadsheet and presented to the executive committee or diversity steering group in the hope that something will change. This is one of the reasons why much activity on D & I has not had the desired and anticipated impact on the business or the individuals within it – a lot of undirected or isolated activity will have a very limited impact.'

Whilst changing an organisational culture can be a very

long-term process (which is not a reason not to start), there are some quick wins to be gained.

Not surprisingly, leadership plays a huge part in any culture change, particularly senior leaders modelling the desired behaviours. In a large professional services company we were working with, a senior partner decided to be open about his mental health condition. He talked of having been hospitalised for a period of time, and being supported by the company, and that on his return he felt his opportunities had not been disadvantaged in any way by this episode.

This gave a very powerful message to everyone that it's OK to be open about mental health – at least in this organisation - and that career progression won't be held back because of it. Employees felt able to share their issues with managers, enabling measures to be put in place before a crisis occurred in some cases.

Many organisations (such as Shell, EY and Lloyds Banking Group) have had campaigns such as 'this is me', where employees have shared their impairments openly, demonstrating the diversity of employees, and encouraging the celebration of difference. A similar campaign run by Channel 4, within a broader data sharing campaign, a key element of which addressed 'what's in it for me?' (if you tell us, we can support you better, raised the rate of people being open about their disability from 2% to 11%. At the same time, they brought in Graeme Whippy, a Business Disability Consultant, to improve their workplace adjustments process.

Having an employee resource network around disability or accessibility can demonstrate the organisation's commitment to equality, whilst feedback from those groups can be implemented and practice improved.

Adding inclusion KPIs to performance management of all leaders (as happens, for example, in Microsoft and HS2) will put inclusion firmly on their agenda, and therefore raise its visibility in the organisation as a whole. It also powerfully states that inclusion isn't just for the EDI team to work on – it's everyone's responsibility.

Offering training programmes around diversity and disability (delivered by disabled people) can raise awareness across the organisation. And internal communications can reinforce positive messages.

Poster campaigns, exhibitions, human libraries, case studies, newsletters, videos and other methods can be used to raise awareness and keep the subject on people's radar.

Having an inclusive culture is essential to the retention of disabled employees, and in creating a climate where they can contribute their skills and thrive in the workplace. It also makes the organisation an attractive place to work – to all candidates, disabled or otherwise.

In a nutshell:

Create an inclusive climate where difference is valued and people feel free to be themselves

"The secret of change is to focus all your energy not on fighting the old but on building the new."

Socrates

Great Way #2: Decide what you need

A vacancy arises, and needs to be filled. Often, the recruiter digs out the job description used last time, and looks for someone who is a double of the person who has just left. They may hope to find someone who has done the same job in the same sector, thinking this will mean there is no need to train the person.

Colin has left. We liked Colin, so what we need is a carbon copy of Colin to replace him. Preferably yesterday.

There are a number of problems with this approach. The first is that you are severely limiting the candidates you will consider, as there may be some great people with transferable skills that you are missing out on. The second is that someone in a similar position in another organisation is unlikely to want a sideways move unless you offer something pretty spectacular that their current employer doesn't. And the third, and arguably the most important, problem is that you are missing an opportunity to review the role to see if it can be changed to better serve the current or future needs of the organisation.

It is essential, therefore, to really think through what is genuinely required for each role. When a vacancy arises, rather than just repeating the criteria from the previous time, or basing it on the previous incumbent, use this as an opportunity to review the role. Is it still relevant? Can it be amended to add more value to the organisation? Perhaps building in new technology or ways of working? Could it include aspects which will future-proof the company?

Think about what qualities the ideal candidate would be able to offer. This is often seen in terms of competencies or experience in a similar role. However, many employers are now placing less emphasis on qualifications and work history, and more emphasis on values and strengths.

Qualifications

For some roles, particular qualifications will be necessary. I wouldn't want an unqualified brain surgeon operating on me, for example! But there has been a trend for recruiters to use qualifications as a first sifting tool even for roles where they aren't relevant. If you have fifty applicants, maybe just eliminate those without a degree? If having a degree isn't necessary for the role, you may well have just excluded the best candidate.

In those cases where a degree is objectively required, how do we assess which degree is better than others? Some employers will only accept degrees from a 'red brick' university, or even insist on Oxbridge graduates. Some will insist on the need for a First.

However, consider two candidates. One from a wealthy privileged background who went to a top public school, had private tutors, went to Oxford and gained a First in their degree. They may well be the best person for the job.
Now consider a second candidate. They grew up in an inner-city area, attending a local run-down state school, and

no-one in their circle of family or friends had ever been to university. They have Dyslexia. Despite this, they worked hard to gain GCSEs and A levels, and got a place at a former Polytechnic where they achieved a 2:1. They may also be the best person for the job.

There will be other considerations around each candidate, of course, but the latter candidate has demonstrated strength, determination and drive, and it could be a huge mistake to discount them purely because of their degree or university.

Essential requirements

Focus only on those qualities that are essential for the role. What does the post-holder really need to be able to do? For example, a delivery driver will clearly need to have a driving licence. However, someone who has some degree of travel within their role may need to be able to move from site to site. This could mean driving, but it could also mean using public transport, or even being driven. Access to Work (a scheme run by the UK government to provide adjustments needed by disabled people in order to work) will usually pay for a driver, when this is the only way an employee can travel.

Requiring the candidate to have a driving licence in these circumstances, quite apart from being illegal (indirect disability discrimination), also means potentially missing out on some great candidates. People with some forms of epilepsy, or sight impairment, or some mental health conditions – or someone who has simply not learned to drive – may have everything you need, and travelling without driving can clearly be addressed.

Because of my annoying inability to sit for any length of time, driving distances is impossible for me. On occasions when I can't use public transport for work-related appointments, I travel lying down in the car, with a driver paid for by Access to Work.

Many qualities are often included in a person specification whether or not they are really needed for that role. For example, the ubiquitous 'team player' seems to appear everywhere. And for many roles it may be important. For many others, it may be more important for the person to be able to work autonomously.

A Data Entry Clerk needs to have great attention to detail, but not necessarily be the life and soul of a party. Being able to avoid being distracted by the team may be more applicable. A coder may not need fantastic 'interpersonal skills' (another ubiquitous requirement) if they work on their own in a cubicle all day.

Culture Fit

Another ubiquitous, if somewhat nebulous, requirement that most employers and recruiters seem to look for is 'culture fit'. What does this actually mean? It will mean different things for different organisations, and different teams and managers within those organisations. If culture means 'the way we do things around here', then looking for culture fit will inevitably mean that 'the way we do things' is never challenged or improved. How does the organisation benefit from a lack of continuous improvement or innovation?

Culture can also include activities outside of work. It may be that a particular team has a drink at the local pub every Friday night with their partners. When recruiting a new member of the team, they may consciously or unconsciously be looking for someone who will fit nicely into that social group. If a candidate isn't a drinker, or isn't keen on socialising with work colleagues, or can't access the local pub, or doesn't have partner, they may not be considered, even if they are the best candidate for the role itself.

One of the dangers of not having a diverse workforce is the likelihood of 'group think'. This is where similar people have similar ideas, views and ways of thinking. Whilst having everyone always agree with each other at every meeting can make for an easy (if incredibly boring) time, it does mean that new ideas, or conflicting views, or different perspectives are rarely heard. It can be difficult for new members, especially if they do have different ideas, to challenge a group unused to being challenged.

Having diverse teams which include people with different life experiences and different thinking styles can avoid the dangers of group think, provided everyone's voice is encouraged to be heard. In this instant, having neuro-diverse people on the team can be incredibly valuable.

At Evenbreak we have a small but incredibly diverse team. It includes a range of impairments, ethnic backgrounds, genders, ages, nationalities, sexual orientations and family circumstances. Our meetings are never dull! Important decisions are never taken lightly, and nearly always include a number of different viewpoints. It requires more thinking and discussion than every suggestion just going through on the nod, but the outcome is much better-quality decisions.

Instead of looking for 'culture fit', look for 'culture add'.

Values

Looking for values is different from culture fit. Values and relevant strengths are the core of what we look for at Evenbreak. For example, whilst all of our candidates identify as being disabled, there is a broad range of ways that disability can be viewed. It's essential for all of the Evenbreak team to subscribe to the social model of disability (see earlier).

We exist, mostly, to challenge the prevailing views of disabled people as objects of pity that employers should feel sorry for, and give them jobs even though they are less able than everyone else. If we employ disabled people who share that view (and some do), we will never successfully change that narrative. The social model, and the human rights model, is fundamental to the way we work together as a team, and the way we work with our employers and candidates, and so it's crucial that all our people share those values.

All organisations have values, whether they are explicit or otherwise. Some businesses have the unspoken value of 'maximum profit is all that matters'. Whatever their policies and mission statements, if this is the prevailing underlying value, it will impact on everything. Management style, hiring decisions, organisational culture. Similarly, for businesses that have values around ethics, integrity, quality, customer service, social impact, environmental sustainability or whatever, those values will also impact on everything, including management style, hiring decisions and organisational culture.

Of course, it's important for those values to be real. By real, I mean actually lived by everyone; guiding behaviour, relationships and decisions. Having a list of values in the company brochure is only meaningful if everyone shares and lives those values; a mismatch will very soon become obvious. And potentially highly damaging. Most things can be taught. Values can be influenced, but this takes much longer. If you recruit people with the values you need, this makes life much easier.

Strengths

Different roles will require different strengths. Like values, strengths can be developed, but finding someone with the strengths the role requires means the role is likely to be performed better. It is much easier to train people in new skills or tasks, but strengths tend to be more innate.

Many hiring managers, thinking it will make life easier, look for candidates who have recent experience of carrying out that particular role in a similar company in the same sector. On the surface, this would seem to make sense. The new recruit will quickly become productive, needing little training. However, bringing in people in this way can be fraught with hidden risks, as we have already seen. If someone has always done a similar job, are they likely to bring new ideas with them? Or challenge the status quo?

For each role you are advertising, think about the personal qualities required to carry it out effectively. These could include creativity, attention to detail, rapport-building, spacial awareness, empathy, objectivity or any others. It makes sense to find people with the strengths that match those needed for the role.

Take Manjit, for example. Manjit thrives around people. She loves listening to others, building a rapport with them and finding solutions to their problems. She has a great ability to remember faces and names, and personal details about people she has met. She is a friendly and approachable person that people warm to.
Then consider Pete. He thrives when given a complex problem to solve. He is great at doing forensic research around the subject and testing different solutions. He is able to retain a large amount of information and can spot connections easily.

Both have some impressive strengths. In a sales role, Manjit is likely to perform really well. In an engineering or software role, Pete is likely to perform really well. However, if you put

Pete into some sales positions, he is less likely to achieve. Manjit is less likely to thrive in a role where contact with other people is limited and much attention to intricate detail is required.

Note that the strengths described are transferable. Manjit may have used her strengths in a therapeutic counselling role previously. But those same strengths will be equally useful in a sales role. Or a customer service role. Or a people management role. You get the idea.

Pete's strengths can also be used in a variety of different roles in different sectors. And if they happen to be disabled people, they still have those strengths. Their condition is only relevant in terms of providing adjustments (should they need any).

Transferable Skills

Like strengths, each role will require certain skills. Most skills are transferable. Someone good at selling photocopiers is also likely to be good at selling holidays. The skills are similar, and the product knowledge can be learned.

Management skills are also transferable. A disabled person who employs support workers or personal assistants may have skills in recruitment, induction, training and performance management. They may also have skills in budgeting and money management. These skills can often be effectively transferred to management roles within the workplace.

There is a disproportionately high number of disabled people who volunteer. Skills developed and honed within voluntary roles can easily be transferred to the workplace. Someone who has worked as a Samaritan volunteer, for instance, is likely to have good listening skills and emotional resilience.

A candidate who has worked in a charity shop will have retail skills. A person who has chaired a board of trustees may well have leadership skills.

When looking for skills, it's important to identify the relevant skill rather than the situation it has been learned in.

Job design

Recruiters often talk about 'the ideal candidate' – it's a phrase I have already used in this book. In reality, of course, it's rare to find an individual who can perform every task required of them to an exactingly high standard. Can you? I know that I carry out some parts of my role better than other parts, and some I do because I have to, not because I'm good at them.

We can sometimes expect candidates to be perfect in every way, and have a range of skills rarely found together in the same person. If a role involves meticulous attention to detail, creative thinking, interpersonal skills and writing reports, it's unlikely that someone will be equally brilliant at all four. A person who has great attention to detail may not be fantastic at creative thinking. Someone great with customers might not be wonderful at writing detailed reports. And so on.

One of the many beauties of having a diverse workforce is the equally diverse range of skills on offer. Playing to those strengths is when the magic happens.

If someone is great at detailed research and analytics, and hates 'brainstorming ideas in a team meeting' or chatting with clients, let them get on with the research while a colleague great at something else does that. If another person is fantastic at coming up with really creative ideas, don't give them data entry work.

That's not to say that, as humans, we only have one skill each; it's about maximising the use of people's talents and passions.

We hired two really talented people as Employer Engagement Managers. Cass and Adam. The role involved both engaging with and supporting existing clients, and introducing Evenbreak to prospective clients. Both activities, on the surface, require similar skills. However, a few weeks into their roles, it became clear that Cass really excels at maintaining great relationships with clients, finding out interesting stories they and their colleagues have to tell about the great inclusive things they are doing, and sharing them on social media. She really doesn't like conversations with clients that involve money.

Adam, however, has little experience of, or interest in, social media. Where he really shines is in engaging with people who are interested in finding effective ways to attract disabled candidates. He loves it when a new client comes on board.

This was an easy one – Adam does all the 'sales' and dropped the account management part of his role, and new clients are passed to Cass, who would then support and nurture them. Now we see the two roles as separate.

It's not always as straightforward as that, of course. And sometimes people want to learn new skills. Everyone will have parts of their role they don't enjoy as much, and often they will just have to get on with it. But it makes no sense to have roles where few are likely to thrive by expecting so many, usually conflicting, strengths.

Job design needs to reflect this. This is relevant whether the person is disabled or not, and is just good talent management. But it also opens up opportunities for disabled people to carry out a role they can excel in, without being expected to do a related task that someone else could carry out.

This is similar to job carving, which also enables people to play to their strengths and focus on the aspects of a role they excel at. For example, if a disabled person (or for that matter, a non-disabled person) applies for a role where they would clearly excel in 90% of the tasks required, but for some reason were unable to carry out the remaining 10%, would you turn them down, or appoint them and have someone else to do that 10%?

Objective criteria

Having identified the essential requirements of the role, in terms of experience, qualifications (if needed), values, strengths and transferable skills, you then have an objective set of criteria with which to target and assess candidates.

The best way to objectively find the best person for the job is to measure them against objective and relevant criteria.

Patel and Yafai (2016)[9] state that, 'In order to employ the right people, it is essential to set objective criteria against which to assess candidates.'

The key work there is 'objective'. Frost (2016)[10] suggests that, 'Many organisations still have questionable criteria that they seek in candidates. They reward those who fit and penalise those who don't.'

Patel and Yafai go on to say, 'In order to make selection effective for both the prospective appointee and the organisation, it needs to be objective and to take into account both the actual and potential competency of an individual to undertake the role to be filled. This can be accomplished in a number of ways. The prerequisite would be to ensure the role is clearly defined and then to identify appropriate skills needed to be able to fulfil the clearly-defined role.'

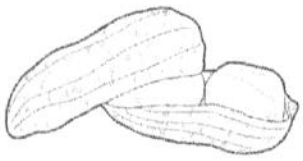

In a nutshell:

Decide objectively what strengths you need the candidate to have before you start looking for them.

"The world we have created is a product of our thinking. It cannot be changed without changing our thinking."

Albert Einstein

Part Two

Attraction

An obvious observation is that if we keep looking in the same places, we'll keep finding the same things. If we want to attract different people, we'll have to use different attraction strategies.

Patel and Yafai (2016)[9] state that, 'Attraction is the process of identifying and encouraging applications from the broadest pool of talent available and potentially willing to join the recruiting organisation. It is in an organisation's best interest to be able to select from the most appropriate/best qualified individuals to undertake the role/function for which a vacancy exists.'

There is a good reason why disabled candidates are hard to attract. Most employers state somewhere that they are "Equal Opportunity Employers". However, disabled candidates have learned, through long and bitter experience, that most aren't - at least where disability is concerned. Too many times to be coincidence, the recruitment process has come to an abrupt end as soon as their impairment becomes apparent (either through mentioning it on application, or because it is visible at interview).

Frost and Kalman (2016)[1] suggest that, 'If you want diversity, you have to convince people you are serious about it, because otherwise they won't even listen, let alone apply.'

Case Study – Fujitsu

Fujitsu wanted to increase the number of disabled applicants for their Graduate, Industrial Placement and Apprenticeships schemes.

The website is often the first contact that applicants will have with Fujitsu. Applicants use the website to find out more about Fujitsu, learn about the available roles, and to make their applications. However, the website was not accessible for all disabled users – in fact, it wasn't easy for anyone to navigate – and it failed to promote Fujitsu as a diverse and inclusive employer.

They revamped the website design to make it clearer and more accessible. There is now simpler signposting on the website and less clutter of information on each page. The text is broken up with images and videos, all using highly contrasting colours. The site is compatible with screen reading software and meets a higher standard of web accessibility. These changes benefit all potential applicants, not just those with disabilities, by making it easier to access information about Fujitsu.

They also improved the content to showcase Fujitsu as an employer that encourages applications from disabled candidates and supports its disabled employees effectively, by adding:

- A 'Creating a Diverse Future' video onto the front page of the website, which promotes their D&I Networks and focuses on Junior Talent
- A whole section about Diversity and Inclusion where they included case studies of disabled employees working at Fujitsu
- Information about how to request reasonable adjustments during the recruitment process
- Details of the awards and recognition they have won in the field of Diversity & Inclusion
- Consistent messages about Fujitsu's belief in the Power of Difference throughout the site
- As a result, they significantly increased the number of applicants who were open about their impairments, and also the number of candidates requesting adjustments.

“Diversity is not the problem;
it’s the solution to the problem.”

Mark Lomas, EDI Manager, HS2

Great Way #3: Be an Inclusive Employer of Choice

If you think dispassionately about your organisation, would you say it's immediately perceived as disability-friendly to the outside world? If not, why would a disabled candidate, who has probably faced countless rejections from other employers, feel safe to apply to work for you?

Yes, you may have a strapline on your adverts that says 'we are an equal opportunities employer', but as we have seen, most disabled people have found that phrase to be fairly meaningless when it comes to, well, equality.

We know that we have to work even harder to attract talented disabled candidates. In recent research we commissioned, carried out by Enactus at University College London[11], we asked over 700 disabled people about the barriers they face when looking for work. 82% of respondents reported that the most pressing problem to them was finding a truly disability-friendly employer, and 15% of respondents say they exclusively apply to disability-friendly employers, with many more seeking openly disability-friendly employers.

Respondents overwhelmingly perceived that there is a lack of understanding by employers. Over 70% rated employers 'very low' with regard to understanding and empathising with the issues they encounter because of their disability.
Whilst disappointing, this means that you have an amazing

opportunity to attract this specific pool of talent. You can really stand out from other employers by ensuring your adverts make it clear you are keen to see candidates' talent first, and that your company (and recruitment process) is accessible and inclusive.

Branding, or 'Employer Value Proposition', is very important when it comes to attracting candidates from new markets, especially in a time (as of writing this) of fairly high employment levels.

Frost and Kalman (2016)[1] state, 'An employer brand is better known as the employee value proposition (EVP), and given that recruiting new staff is a significant investment, it's important to make it as efficient and effective as possible. An EVP is the mix of characteristics, benefits and ways of working in an organisation. Sometimes it's referred to as the deal stuck between an organisation and employee in return for their contribution and performance. Organisations come unstuck when their EVP doesn't speak to their (new) target audience.'

They also remind us that, 'It's inauthentic to communicate an EVP that is undermined by the reviews your own people leave on social media sites such as glassdoor.com.'

Sweeney and Bothwick (2016)[6] state that, 'Research shows us that it costs a company more to attract and hire someone if they have a weak employer brand.'
It's a good idea to ensure that imagery used on your careers site, website and other promotional material, reflects a

diverse range of people (without being tokenistic, of course).

Seeing visibly disabled people at all levels of the organisation sends a positive signal that disabled people can thrive in your company.

External Accreditation

External accreditation or recognition can also strongly indicate your commitment to disability inclusion. There are a number of these around. These are some in the UK, for instance:

Disability Confident

This is a (free) government-run initiative aimed at helping employers become, as the name suggests, more confident around disability. It replaces the previous Positive about Disability Symbol (also known as the "Two Ticks Symbol").

The scheme has three levels:

Disability Confident Committed – the organisation is beginning to look at disability inclusion, and is committed to making at least one of the suggested improvements in the following 12 months. The company registers on the scheme, but is not externally assessed.

Disability Confident Employer – the organisation has taken action to remove a number of disabling barriers in their recruitment and employment practices, and have embedded a range of inclusive and accessible policies and practices. This is also self-assessed.

Disability Confident Leader – the organisation has achieved a high standard of inclusion and accessibility and is helping other organisations to follow suit. This level is externally and independently assessed.

At the time of writing, the Disability Confident scheme has mixed reviews in terms of its genuine impact and the way it is assessed, but at the very least, displaying your level of commitment indicates to disabled candidates that disability inclusion is on your radar. I hope the scheme will be further improved over time.

Disability Standard

The Disability Standard is a whole-organisation disability management audit developed by Business Disability Forum to help organisations measure and improve on performance for disabled customers, clients or service users, employees and stakeholders.

It helps organisations to measure and improve their progress towards becoming disability-smart, and helps them check how disability-smart their organisation is, across the whole of the business. Ten business areas are covered in the evaluation:

- Commitment
- Know-how
- Adjustments

- Recruitment
- Retention
- Products and services
- Suppliers and Partners
- Communication
- Premises
- IT

Mindful Employer

Mindful Employer is a UK wide initiative run by Devon Partnership NHS Trust. Providing employers with easy access to professional workplace mental health training, information and advice; they help empower organisations – large or small – to take a lead in supporting the mental wellbeing of staff. Having the 'Mindful Employer' logo on your website confirms your commitment to supporting mental health within your workforce.

Work With Me

The #WorkWithMe community invites you to make disability your business – a new movement powered by Virgin Media, Scope and Valuable. #WorkWithMe is a network of businesses that support each other in becoming more inclusive for disabled people. It is a growing community committed to changing employment practices, customer relations and brand value.

The Valuable 500

The Valuable 500 is a global movement putting disability on the business leadership agenda. The aim is for 500 national and multinational, private sector corporations to be the tipping-point for change and to unlock the business, social and economic value of people living with disabilities across the world.

Clear Assured

Owned and developed by The Clear Company, Clear Assured is a recognised Diversity and Inclusion standard. The HR software gives Diversity and HR teams clear direction, effective tools and benchmarking capability. Clear Assured sets direction, showing the areas that require focus in order to make the biggest impact and continually improve.

Used across a variety of business sectors, it measures progress and offers accreditation, educates through sharing the latest thinking on inclusion, empowers supply chains and offers online support from experts.

Awards

Entering awards may seem a bit like looking for glorification, and some organisations shy away from them. However, entering or being nominated for awards can also raise your profile in terms of your performance in this area. New awards are appearing all the time, and here are a few I'm aware of:

Recruitment Industry Disability Initiative (RIDI) Awards

Aimed at recruitment companies and in-house recruiters, the free-to-enter RIDI awards celebrate and share inclusive and accessible practice in recruitment. A number of categories celebrate disability confident recruitment, from those at the very beginning of their journey to organisations demonstrating best practice and knowledge sharing in their sector.

Disability Smart Awards

Run by the Business Disability Forum, these annual awards celebrate best practice across all areas of business.

Inclusive Companies Awards

These awards celebrate achievements in inclusion and diversity across the full spectrum of diversity, and reward individuals and companies for going above and beyond to create a more diverse and inclusive society.

Inclusive Top 50 UK Employers

The Inclusive Top 50 UK Employers is the first and only index of its kind – an annual list of the nation's most inclusive companies.
As well as displaying these accreditations and awards (there will be equivalents in other countries) on your careers site, there are additional ways of demonstrating your commitment to disability inclusion.

Making it clear what you offer as an inclusive employer can be key in encouraging disabled candidates to apply. Things that you might take for granted, such as flexible working patterns (amazingly, some employers still don't offer this for roles which could be worked flexibly and/or remotely). Offering workplace adjustments (which you have to offer by law, but making it explicit can be reassuring to candidates who have often met resistance in this area). If you have a Disability Group. And anything else which might re-assure potential disabled applicants.

It can be powerful to share the voices of existing disabled employees, through written case studies with photos, or through video. Employees talking about how they feel valued, the career progression opportunities they have access to, and the workplace adjustments they have benefitted from, can be helpful in showing candidates what their experience might be like. Graeme Whippy, a great Business Disability Consultant, has this mantra – 'Show the world that you're a brilliant employer for the disabled people you've already got, and then you'll attract more of them.'

Also, senior endorsement of disability inclusion strategies, and a statement about why it is important for your organisation to employ disabled people can feel welcoming.

In a nutshell:

Make sure you establish credibility so that disabled people have the confidence to apply for your jobs

"If you haven't got the best talent, you're not going to be the best, if you're not representing properly the available pool of talent then you're missing an opportunity."

Alex Wilmot-Sitwell, EMEA President,
Bank of America Merrill Lynch

Great Way #4: Effective Job Design

The world of work is changing.

Traditionally, most jobs have involved a similar working pattern. Full time. Five days a week (Monday to Friday). 9.00am to 5.00pm. In a work setting – office, factory, shop, whatever. Exceptions being shift work, such as in hospitals, emergency services, care work and the like, but even these also tend to have their own patterns of work, including around 40 hours a week.

This rigid style of working can cause problems for many people. Hordes of people starting and finishing work at around the same time creates the nightmare of the ridiculously-named 'rush hour'. Parents have to drop their children off at school at the same time they should be arriving at work.

Workers are unable to do the things they need to do because they are at work when the services they need are open.

Forty hours is an arbitrary number of hours. Some people (junior doctors or small business owners, for example) work far more than that, others work far fewer.

Banks recognised that have branches open between 9.30am and 3.00pm was not useful, and telephone and internet banking became popular. Shops open for much longer. We have almost become a 24-hour economy, which has advantages and disadvantages that are outside the scope of this book to explore.

During the Covid-19 pandemic, many people unexpectedly found themselves having to work from home. Often in roles that employers had previously assumed couldn't be carried out effectively unless on-site. Ironically, many disabled candidates will have been told the roles they are applying couldn't be done from home, although since then, it has become apparent that many roles can.

A number of employees – disabled and otherwise – decided there were some sound benefits to working from home. Less time spent commuting. More time with family. And employers learned that people working from home could be just as productive – if not more so – than they were in the workplace. Home-working is now seen as a valid option for many roles, whether for all or part of the week.

Are your current jobs designed with this new world of work in mind?

It may be the role could be carved into two quite different part-time roles. Or perhaps all or part of it could be done remotely.

When a vacancy occurs, either through someone leaving or if it's a newly-created role, it's a great opportunity to ensure the job role is designed for today's and tomorrow's needs rather than assuming 'how we've always done things' is the only, or best way.

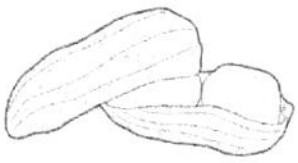

In a nutshell:
Focus on strengths and attitudes and only essential skills, experience and qualifications. The latter three can be gained over time, the former two are unlikely to change.

“The flower that blooms in adversity is the most rare and beautiful of all.”

Mulan (Walt Disney)

Great Way #5: Find your Target Audience

If you advertise in the same places, you'll attract the same kind of candidates. There may be nothing wrong with those places, or those candidates, but if your current talent pool isn't diverse, you'll need to find additional, and different, ways of finding talent.

Specifically targeting candidates who may not traditionally apply is vital if you wish to attract diverse talent. There are a number of ways of doing this.

Disability journals

Some disability magazines offer the opportunity to advertise jobs. The benefit of doing this is that you have a ready-made audience of the group you are trying to attract. In addition, that audience will have confidence in organisations which have paid to advertise in a disability magazine. Having a presence in disability media enhances your reputation as an inclusive organisation to potential customers, too.

This can be quite expensive, depending on the journal, so you may wish to use this method for senior roles, or volume roles, such as a call centre or a new site.

Specialist job boards

It's difficult for me to be objective about this one, as I run a specialist disability job board! However, this does give me in-depth experience in this area.

Disabled candidates tell us that if they see a role advertised on Evenbreak, they have the confidence to apply. An employer paying to advertise their vacancies on a job board specifically targeting disabled candidates demonstrates they have a genuine commitment to inclusion and won't automatically discriminate against candidates because of an impairment which is not relevant.

I would hope that all specialist disability job boards would be completely accessible (you would be surprised how many aren't!). Evenbreak is built and maintained to the highest possible standards of accessibility, meaning that those candidates who are unable to access the majority of job boards can access ours, enabling a much broader range of candidates.

Working with partners

Up and down the country there are thousands of organisations who help disabled people find work. Sometimes these are large, national charities who may focus on a specific impairment (e.g. for blind or Deaf people), or pan-disability. There are many, many smaller, usually local or regional, organisations which may be charities, social enterprises or others.

Disabled people-led organisations (DPLOs) can be an amazing source of local talent. Run by disabled people, these organisations will not only be able to find suitable candidates for you, but will usually also help you with the recruitment process, and offer continuing support after the candidate is appointed.

Frost and Kalman (2016)[1] agree, and suggest, 'Think even harder and more creatively about who you can partner with to access talent sources that hitherto have been untapped by your recruitment function. There exists a whole infrastructure out there in the voluntary, quasi-government, charity as well as commercial sectors dedicated to connecting diverse talent to opportunity.'

Some areas have umbrella bodies for DPLOs (for example, Inclusion Scotland and Inclusion London), and most areas have voluntary sector support organisations. There are national campaigns too – for example Leonard Cheshire's Change 100 programme, and Beco's #StealOurStaff. There will be similar campaigns in other countries, too.

When recruiting staff and volunteers for the London Paralympics in 2012, great use was made of local community groups. Frost (2014)[6] tells us, 'On the supply side we undertook unprecedented outreach and partnered with hundreds of community organisations ... They could reach talent quicker, more efficiently and effectively than we could.'

Case Study – John Lewis Partnership

The John Lewis Partnership won the 'Getting Started' category in the RIDI awards in 2018 and became a Disability Confident Leader in early 2019. Their motivation for focusing on disability inclusion was the realisation that having more disabled partners (colleagues) would help the organisation to have a much better understanding of how to identify where disabled customers might face barriers.

The John Lewis Partnership was the first major retailer to advertise their vacancies on Evenbreak. Carole Donaldson, JLP's Resourcing Manager, speaking at an event sharing their best practice, stated, "At first, we questioned which roles to post on Evenbreak - but then soon came to the realisation that *every* role needs to be as accessible as possible: true inclusivity makes it easier for everyone."

Using Evenbreak's specialist job board and best practice portal, and training managers in disability and inclusion, were instrumental in both winning the award, and in gaining Disability Confident Leader status.

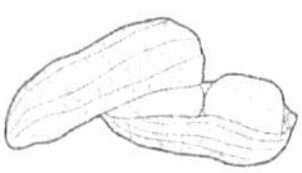

In a nutshell:
If you look in the same places, you'll find the same kind of candidates. Look in different places to find new candidates

"The days of pick and mix inclusion are over. You can no longer be 'diverse-ish'"

Caroline Casey, Valuable 500

Great Way #6: Write Inclusive Job Adverts

When recruiting, your job advert is your first chance to attract talented individuals to your roles. This is also the first impression that candidates will get of your business and you know what they say about first impressions! A well-written job advert will provide candidates with a great first impression, both of the role and your company.

Remember that many candidates may already be in work, so you have to make the role enticing enough for them to risk making the move.

Booth (2016)[12] offers general advice on writing job adverts specifically for autistic candidates, but this is good practice for all candidates. She suggests:

'Job adverts and job descriptions can minimise barriers to autistic applicants by:

- being clear and concise, using straightforward language
- avoiding jargon and unnecessary information
- including information about support, adjustments and the workplace environment
- including only job requirements that are objectively necessary
- avoiding specifying personality types required, such as "outgoing" or "team player"; instead specifying job roles such as "serving customers".'

Establishing Credibility

As discussed in a previous chapter, if you have gained any recognition for inclusion, make sure candidates know. For example, being a Mindful Employer, a Disability Confident Employer/Leader, a #WorkWithMe member or having the Disability Standard. Other diversity and inclusion accreditations are good too, such as the Stonewall Workplace Equality Index (LGBTQ+ people can be disabled too!).

Similarly, if you have content demonstrating your credibility, offer links to it.

The more you do in this area, the more confidence disabled candidates will have in applying for your roles.

Elements of the advert

Commonly, job adverts can read more like a job description than an advert. A job advert is not the same as a job description and doesn't need to include every element of the role, just enough to encourage the right people to apply. These are the elements you might consider including:

Job Title

It's important to ensure the job title accurately reflects the role, otherwise you may attract unsuitable candidates, or mislead candidates who may not stay long in their post if it doesn't live up to expectations. Being too creative here can backfire – candidates tend to search for the job title they are looking for, and may not find a whacky one. Consider what terms your ideal candidate might search for.

So, for example, if you want a Marketing Manager don't ask for 'Wizard of Light Bulb Moments'. If you are looking for a Website Manager, don't ask for a 'Digital Overlord'.

Salary

Most employers avoid including salary information in job adverts, using the ubiquitous "competitive" or "negotiable". Whilst there may be good reasons not to specify the salary, including a salary within your advert is probably one of the quickest ways of improving the number and quality of responses that your advert receives.

On average, Reed have found that a vacancy with a fixed salary receives 90% more applications than one with a hidden or negotiable salary.[13]

Research by Hays[14] revealed that the top two criteria for candidates to filter by when searching for a job were salary and location. With current technology, many roles which used to require regular travel, may not now. It's important to mention if the role can be carried out remotely, otherwise many potentially suitable candidates may not apply.

A competitive salary helps to attract candidates and will

also filter out any applicants with unrealistic salary expectations. Additionally, it gives applicants an idea of the seniority level of the role which means that you are more likely to end up with a greater number of more relevant candidates.

Opening Paragraph

As with any advertising, it's important to grab your target's attention and interest quickly. They may well be looking through large numbers of adverts, and you need to stand out from the crowd so they will read on.

A study published in the Journal of Business and Psychology[15] found that job adverts that focus on the candidate's needs receive 3 times as many applications and a higher quality candidate pool.

The candidate – any candidate, not just disabled ones – will want to know what kind of employer you are. This is what will draw candidates to read further (or make them scroll down to the next advert). Not just a re-hash of your 'About Us' page, but something that really makes people want to work for you.

Ask yourself why talented candidates would choose you over other employers to work for. What's in it for them? Better still, ask existing employees why they love working for you (including, of course, disabled employees) and include their answers in your opening 'pitch'. Your brand alone may not be enough. There are many other exciting brands around.

Include three to five reasons why your company and this role are attractive, exciting and enticing. Make a concise and compelling case for why the right candidates should apply for this position.

Role Description

The description of the role can be brief. For example, if you are advertising for an accountant, you don't need to list all the tasks an accountant carries out – suitable candidates will already know that. A brief overview of the three or four main objectives will be enough.

Make sure that the description is accurate, so that candidates have enough information to self-select. We have discovered that, generally speaking, disabled candidates tend only to apply for jobs they know they can do. Unfortunately, they are also often good at selecting themselves out of jobs they could also do.

Another benefit of being specific about the kinds of tasks the job entails will enable disabled candidates to assess if the role is right for them. Will they need physical strength? Will the role involve a lot of standing or walking? Could they do these tasks with adjustments?

An indication of the level of the role is useful (is it operational? Managerial? Strategic?), as is something about context.

So, instead of a vague description of 'content creation', you might say 'creation of content for blogs, newsletters and social media to raise awareness of our environmentally-friendly products'.

What you Offer

This is one of the most important parts of the job advert and is where you can really set yourself apart from other employers.

Whilst it is important for all candidates to have information about the kind of employer you are and what perks are available (career progression opportunities, bonuses, annual leave, pension schemes, private healthcare, for example), disabled candidates may well also be interested in aspects such as:

- Flexible/remote working
- Accessible buildings
- Close parking
- Employee resource networks
- Buddy schemes
- Mentoring opportunities
- Workplace adjustments

Ideally you will have a page on your website (and/or your profile page on the job board) which explains all this, and you can link to it from your advert. This may need to include national variations if you are multi-national.

What can work well is to have a short video from a very senior person saying why you value disabled employees, and then some videos of disabled employees talking about their role and the support and opportunities they have received, along with any external recognition you have (Disability Confident status, relevant awards won, etc.)

What you Need

Like the role description, this needs to be factual and accurate. Make sure you are not asking for qualities that are not vital to the role.

No job requires a degree only from Oxford or Cambridge. Or a first. See earlier about the need for degrees.

Some jobs really do require a driving licence. If the role involves delivering products, or driving a goods vehicle, then the post-holder needs a driving licence, and it's fine to ask for one. If the role requires travel between sites, then the requirement is, well, for the candidate to be able to travel between sites. This could mean driving, being driven or using public transport (don't forget Access to Work can help with this).

Strengths v. skills

Most job adverts I see list the skills required, and don't mention strengths.

Do include the strengths you are looking for. These are the

qualities a person has – the (usually innate) traits that are difficult to train someone in. Things like attention to detail, the ability to create rapport quickly, creative thinking. These abilities can be taught, but not easily.

Skills can usually be taught. You may want someone who already has the skills, so you don't need to train them, and that's fine too. Consider whether the candidate needs experience at using those skills specifically within your sector or environment, or whether the skills are transferable from other settings.

For example, skills in managing people are similar whatever the sector. Someone who has managed a project in a voluntary capacity, or managed personal assistants in a care support capacity, will have skills which can be transferred.

Be specific, too. 'Communication skills', for example, is too broad. A Deaf person might be superb at written communication. A blind person may be brilliant on the telephone.

Avoid the ubiquitous requirements which seem to appear in almost every job advert. Does the candidate really need to be a 'team player' if they are based in a cubicle doing data entry? Do they need 'great interpersonal skills' if they are not interacting with people?

When LOCOG (the London Organising Committee of the Olympic and Paralympic Games) were trying to attract a diverse range of applicants to work on the Olympics, they redesigned job descriptions to 'focus on skills and competences, not "evidence of experience" which would be a subtle, often unconscious way, that diverse talent was often filtered out of the process.' In order to help candidates present themselves favourably, LOCOG also laid on CV workshops[10].

Stick to the strengths and skills that are vital for the candidate to have – anything else is fluff, and risks turning great candidates off.

Describe the Process

As we know, recruitment processes can have differing impacts on certain groups of people. Candidates will want to know what the next steps are, and what the process will involve.

It's important that candidates know what assessment methods will be used. In an ideal world, your assessment methods won't completely rely on CVs and interviews (see later chapters on assessment methods).

Whatever methods you do use, it's useful for candidates to know, so they can be prepared for them, and ask for any relevant adjustments they might need in order to participate on a level playing field.

Inclusion Statement

Inclusion statements need to be more than a formal statement that you intend to comply with equality legislation. They should be welcoming, and let candidates know that you value diversity and their application will be taken seriously if they have the qualities you are looking for.

Offer Adjustments

Offering adjustments throughout the whole recruitment process is in your interests as much as the candidates'.

Make it clear in your advert that asking for adjustments will not disadvantage the candidate in any way. The following chapter gives further information on this, and advice on wording.

Call to Action

You would be surprised at how many job adverts don't include a call to action! The candidate needs to know what to do next.

This could be as simple as 'email or call [name] on xxx for further information and an application pack', or 'click apply now for more information'.

It's useful to give a named person and their email address and telephone number (some candidates will prefer one or the other method of communication) that people can contact for further information. This may be around asking for adjustments, or finding out more about the role to decide if it's worth applying for. Whilst this may sound resource-intensive, it can save many unsuitable applications from being submitted, and can also let you know in good time if any candidates do need adjustments.

Here is an example from Channel 4:

> ALTERNATIVE APPLICATION FORMATS:
> If you are unable to complete a written application form, we want to make the process of applying for one of our opportunities right for you as an individual. If needed we are happy to consider alternative formats of the application form.
>
> For example, you could arrange a phone call with 4Talent for you to speak your answers and a member of the team can scribe, or if you'd like to create a five-minute YouTube video/voice recording, these are also options available. If you have a different alternative, we really welcome your suggestions to ensure you have a fair chance of applying.
>
> Take a look at our access page for more information, which you'll find by clicking here. If you would like to apply for an opportunity at 4Talent and we can help to make that process simpler for you, please email us at 4Talent@channel4.co.uk or call *name* on 0207 XXX XXXX.

In a nutshell:
Make sure your job adverts are welcoming to disabled candidates, and accurate – so people can self-select

"Diversity: the art of thinking independently together"

Malcolm Forbes

Great Way #7: Offer Adjustments Throughout

It is really important that candidates feel able to ask for any adjustments they might need, without fearing this will put them at disadvantage, at each and every stage in the recruitment process. Without necessary adjustments they will not be able to adequately demonstrate their strengths, and will be at a disadvantage when compared with other candidates.

It may be that a candidate doesn't need any adjustments in the application process, but does for the interview or assessment part of the process. If they didn't initially ask for adjustments, it shouldn't preclude them for asking for something later on.

In Evenbreak's "Barriers to Employment" research[11], it was found that, 'The most apparent issue appears to be the lack of information in job advertisements regarding available adjustments for the applicant or workplace policies regarding disabled employees. Almost 80% of respondents said this occurred regularly or always.'

In order for you to attract and accurately assess disabled candidates, they need to be able to apply on an equal footing, which means removing any barriers. And they need to know that asking for adjustments won't limit their likelihood of success in any way.

Some employers will say something along the lines of "if you are disabled and need any reasonable adjustments, please let us know". This puts the candidate in a dilemma. If they let you know they need adjustments, they are letting you know they are disabled right at the start. And the word 'reasonable' implies a legalistic definition – who decides what is 'reasonable'? And how should they let you know?

Rather than making it sound like an unwelcome legal obligation, why not make them available for every candidate, and say something along the lines of:

"We really want you to be able to shine in this application so we can see what your strengths are. We offer [*application requirement*] in alternative formats and can be flexible around our process. Please call [*name*] on [*telephone number*] or email him/her on [*email address*] for an informal chat about how we can give you the best opportunity to show us your suitability."

This means if there is an online test or application form, they can ask for different formats, or more time, or whatever they might need, without making it a big deal. It also means non-disabled candidates can ask for what they might need.

It may well be that no adjustments are needed at application stage, so it is important to repeat this offer in the next stage, and every stage throughout the process.

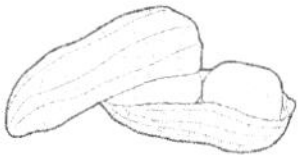

In a nutshell:

Make it easy for candidates to ask for adjustments at any point in the process, without fearing it may harm their chances

"You think the only people who are people, are the people who look and think like you. But if you walk the footsteps of a stranger, you'll learn things you never knew, you never knew."

Pocahontas (Walt Disney)

Part Three

Assessment

Great Way #8: To CV or not to CV

In the interests of openness, I have to declare at this point that I'm not a huge fan of CVs. In some circumstances it can be useful to know what qualifications a candidate has, and what work experience they have had, but CVs rarely accurately reflect their skills or potential.

A CV can give many opportunities for unconscious (and conscious) bias. Someone's name can give an impression of ethnicity, or gender (someone called John is far more likely to be shortlisted than someone called Mohammed or Susan, for example). Their address might indicate the kind of area they live in (the 'rough area of town' or the middle-class suburban estate).

The school they went to will give irrelevant information (c.g. single sex schools, or schools for SEND (special educational needs and disabled) pupils). The school might be a well-known public school, or an under-funded inner city comprehensive. The dates they attended will indicate their age. As will reference to 'O' levels as opposed to GCSEs.

The university, if they attended one, may be a Russell Group red brick university or a former polytechnic.
Their work history is just that – historical. It makes no

mention of potential. And if hobbies are mentioned, they may be made up (people tend to write what they think will impress) or not be relevant.

Very little of the information about the candidate mentioned above gives any indication or evidence about their suitability for a future job.

By its very nature, a CV is a historic document. It describes the education and work opportunities the candidate has been able to access. If they have not had access to the same educational or work opportunities as other candidates due to circumstances or discrimination, they will be hugely disadvantaged in a recruitment process that relies too heavily on CVs.

Let me introduce you to Elaine (a real person, but not her real name). Elaine's CV was of the kind that is usually immediately rejected. In her mid-forties, Elaine had had a large number of jobs, none of which had lasted longer than a few weeks. There were long gaps between the jobs, which grew increasingly longer as her CV prevented her from being hired. Someone who never stays in a job longer than a few weeks can seem like a huge risk, and recruiters are understandably wary.

Elaine is bright, picks up new skills quickly, is highly motivated and rarely, if ever, has time off sick. She is profoundly Deaf, and has been so all her life. She found that managers and colleagues in her various workplaces did not put much effort in to finding the best ways to communicate with her, so either she didn't have the information she needed to carry out her job effectively and failed, or she felt isolated and left.

Her CV did not reflect her qualities, it merely demonstrated the incompetence of previous employers. Having found an employer willing to make minor changes to the way they work, she has been successfully employed for the past six years.

Another example is Amir (also not his real name). His CV is another that would ring alarm bells with most recruiters very early on. Despite having three degrees in unrelated and impressive subjects, and with a number of incredibly useful skills, Amir has been unemployed for more than ten years. Recruiters are unlikely to shortlist a candidate with no recent work experience.

The reason Amir has not worked for so long, despite his impressive abilities, is because he does not perform well at interviews. A bit of an under-statement, really. He is autistic, and doesn't understand the social games that need to be played in interviews. We'll return to Amir in the next chapter on interviews.

However, the gap in his CV bears no relation to his ability to do the job he is applying for; it just demonstrates that traditional recruitment processes don't work for him. He has tried leaving the dates off his work history, but it makes little difference. Recruiters draw their own conclusions to CVs with no dates attached.

You may be shouting at this book right now, and telling me that some recruiters understand the issue of unconscious bias (or as I like to call it, bias), and are now using blind CVs. This certainly helps – certainly removing the name, gender, ethnicity, age and address from the CV can remove clues which could lead to bias. But I'm afraid the same issues around work history and qualifications remain. And the human brain abhors gaps in information and will attempt to fill them in by guessing. So blind CVs can be self-defeating.

If you are one of those recruiters whose jaw drops to the floor at the very thought of not using CVs (and brace yourself – the other sacred part of recruitment, interviews, isn't safe either), chapter 10 gives you some great alternatives.

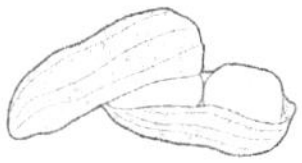

In a nutshell:
Be aware that CVs may disadvantage some disabled candidates, and not demonstrate their true qualities and potential

"When it comes to choosing a candidate, [traditional] interviews are as much use as flipping a coin."

Richard Nisbett,
Professor of Social Psychology,
University of Michigan

Great Way #9: Effective Interviews

I debated on whether or not to include this chapter, as in most circumstances (there will be exceptions) interviews are pretty poor indicators of future performance with any candidate, let alone with disabled candidates. At Evenbreak we no longer use interviews as part of our internal recruitment process (see case study in next chapter).

We know that traditional job interviews are poor predictors of future job performance. Candidates tend to give the answers that are being looked for, and interviewers are likely to pick the people they like rather than those with the most potential.

Despite their popularity, traditional interviews have been largely discredited. Attractive and charismatic candidates aren't necessarily the best fit for the job, but we often unconsciously assume they are.

In a study conducted by LinkedIn Talents Solutions in 2018[16] which surveyed 8,815 talent acquisition professionals and hiring managers, respondents noted the bias problem in traditional interviews as well as their limited ability to assess soft skills and weaknesses.

Respondents felt that traditional interviews fail for the following reasons:

Assessing candidate soft skills (63%)
Understanding candidate weaknesses (57%)

Bias of interviewers (42%)
Too long a process (36%)
Not knowing best questions to ask (18%)

Nisbett (2015)[17] suggests that 'Extroverts in general do better in interviews than introverts, but for many if not most jobs, extroversion is not what we're looking for.'

Research that Jason Dana and his colleagues conducted in 2013[18] shows that the problem with interviews is worse than that of irrelevance. They can be harmful, undercutting the impact of other, more valuable information about interviewees. They state, 'In addition to the vast evidence suggesting that un- structured interviews do not provide incremental validity, we provide direct evidence that they can harm accuracy. ...Our simple recommendation for those who make screening decisions is not to use them.'

Dana (2017)[19] carried out experiments to test the accuracy of interviews against other methods in predicting future performance, and says, 'In one experiment, we had student subjects interview other students and then predict their grade point averages for the following semester. The prediction was to be based on the interview, the student's course schedule and his or her past G.P.A. (We explained that past G.P.A. was historically the best predictor of future grades at their school.) In addition to predicting the G.P.A. of the interviewee, our subjects also predicted the performance of a student they did not meet, based only on that student's course schedule and past G.P.A.
In the end, our subjects' G.P.A. predictions were

significantly more accurate for the students they did not meet. The interviews had been counterproductive.'

An easy way to test your assessment methods is to retrospectively compare career performance with assessment centre performance.

However, it seems likely that at least for the foreseeable future, most employers and recruiters are wedded to the idea of using interviews as a large part, if not all, of the selection process.

Like the CV, ask yourself if an interview is really the best way to assess a candidate's suitability for a role (see next chapter for alternatives).

If you must use an interview – and there may be good reasons for this – it is better to use it in conjunction with other assessment methods and ensure the hiring decision isn't made purely on the candidate's performance at interview.

Do you remember Amir from the last chapter? He doesn't understand that a large unwritten part of the interview is for the candidate to appear likeable and friendly, and the main object of the exercise isn't to convince the interviewer that you are the best person for the job, but to convince them to like you, and that you're a great person for them to work with.

A question such as "Why do you want this job?" is correctly

translated by most candidates as “This is your opportunity to flatter the panel about their organisation, and tell them why your skills mean you would thrive there.” Someone like Amir is likely to take the question at face value, and may say, “Because you have a vacancy and I need a job”.

If asked to “Tell me something about yourself,” (a very common opening question at interviews, designed, oddly, to put candidates at their ease), Amir struggles to see the relevance of the question. He may tell you his height, weight and eye colour. Or when he was born and where his parents lived. Or, more likely, he will say something like, “That’s a really stupid question – why don’t you tell me what you want to know, and I’ll tell you?” He thinks he’s being helpful, the recruiter thinks he’s being rude, and ten years later he is still unemployed.

Of course, it isn’t just autistic candidates who are disadvantaged by interviews. They really don’t work for anyone who isn’t, well, good at blagging at interviews. Which is most people, really. Sitting in front of a bunch of strangers firing questions at you probably isn’t the most effective way to encourage anyone to perform at their best.

Candidates who are shy, or introverts, or have hearing difficulties, or learning difficulties, or lack confidence, or have a speech impairment, or who are anxious are all unlikely to shine at interviews. But they may be the best person to fill the role you currently need to fill.

Relying solely on interviews means you are likely to appoint the person who has the best skills at being interviewed, not necessarily the best skills for carrying out the job in question.

Patel, J. & Yafai[9] suggest that 'History shows us that it is common for recruiters [in interviews] to be more comfortable with individuals who look like them and behave like them than with those who do not. This approach, as has been proven many times, can often lead to a whole organisation becoming almost clone-like.'

However, it may be that you are stuck with using interviews. And for a very small number of roles, they may have some value. So how can we make them as inclusive and accessible as possible? Here are some actions you may wish to consider.

Before the interview:

Ensure the venue is as accessible as possible, and that all panel members are trained in inclusive interview techniques.

Make sure candidates are given adequate notice, and therefore time to prepare, preferably by post and/or email. Be clear about start and end times, so they know how long the interview is likely to last.

Give detailed information about the venue – directions to get there (by public transport and by driving), carparking information, and how accessible the venue is. For some candidates it can be helpful to include photographs of the entrance to the building, the reception area and the interview room.

Encourage candidates to advise you of any adjustments they might need, with examples, and be clear on how they should do this.

Describe the format of the interview, who will be on the panel (how many people, name, job titles etc), and again for some candidates, photographs of the panel might be helpful.

For some candidates it can be helpful to know the questions in advance. If you feel this is a step too far, perhaps just reassure them that the questions will be straightforward, and only relevant to the role being applied for.

If any additional assessment methods are to be used on the day of the interview, such as written or technical tests, or a presentation, be clear about what these involve so the candidate will know if they need to ask for adjustments for those too.

Give details of anything you need the candidate to bring with them (for example, if they can bring notes or a companion with them into the interview), and dress code. The latter might sound obvious to most people, but deciding what to wear can be an enormous source of anxiety for some people.

Booth (2016)[12] reminds us that, 'The benefits of these measures will be lost if the interview does not follow the format notified in advance: for example, if it starts late, if requests for adjustments are ignored or if test questions are printed in a different format from the practice papers.'

Sometimes events are out of our control, and plans do change. Make sure that any unavoidable changes are communicated to the candidate in good time, and alternative arrangements described in detail.

During the interview:

Make sure the questions are straightforward, jargon-free and relevant. Other than for very specific roles (maybe an author of children's books?), there really is no room for "If you were an animal, what would you be and why?" type questions.

The interviewers should ensure that candidates are evaluated purely on their ability to do the job, not by irrelevant social factors such as amount of eye-contact, or how much they fidget.

Whilst many interviews are competency-based, it may be that some disabled candidates have not had access to work opportunities where they will have been able to demonstrate their competence.

Sweeney and Bothwick (2016)[6] tell us, 'Some forward-thinking companies have started to move on from competency-based interviews which look at previous experience in certain situations to strength-based interviews to find the most suitable person for a job based on what that person enjoys doing and is therefore good at.'

Elsewhere we have discussed the benefits of looking at strengths rather than skills, and it makes sense to use the interview to explore this too.

It may be helpful for some candidates to be able to bring a support worker or other companion, take time to acclimatise to the room before the interview starts and be given time to process questions and formulate answers.

After the interview:

It is good practice to have a panel of (diverse) interviewers rather than a single person, so the hiring decision is shared. Frost and Kalman (2016)[1] suggest, "Mixed panels can bring transparency and cognitive rigour to selection. To maximise their effectiveness, have individual panel members come together only after they have individually reviewed the candidates. This will decrease the risk of groupthink and increase insights from different perspectives.'

Scoring candidates individually against a pre-agreed set of relevant criteria, and then comparing notes after the interviews are completed, means that a robust discussion can be had.

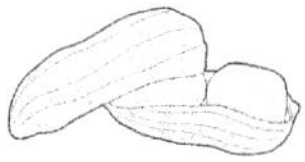

In a nutshell:

If you have to use interviews, make sure they are as relevant and accessible as possible

"If you always do what you've always done,
you'll always get what you've always got"

Anon

Great Way #10: Offer Alternative Assessment Methods

Assessment methods should aim to objectively assess the ability or potential for each candidate to do the tasks involved in the job being filled.

I've suggested that CVs and interviews aren't usually the most effective ways to assess candidates' suitability for a given role, but what are the alternatives?

Alternatives to the traditional CV

Application Forms:

Many organisations no longer accept CVs, and offer an application form instead. This can be more inclusive, as at least every candidate's submission is in a similar format. Booth (2016)[12] suggests that, 'Job application forms can minimise barriers [for autistic applicants] by making them straightforward, no jargon or unnecessary questions, the option of submitting the applications online or on hard copy and space to request further information and adjustments.'

However, if the application form just replicates the format of a CV (name, address, work history with dates, qualifications with dates, etc), then the barriers associated with traditional CVs remain.

On the other hand, if a few, very focused questions are asked (see later), and the personal details removed before shortlisting, this can be a useful method of gaining relevant information which helps with the sifting and shortlisting decisions.

Blind CVs:

Removing personal data which implies gender, age, race, disability and so on from CVs is certainly a step in the right direction in terms of reducing the opportunities for (conscious or unconscious) bias. However, blind CVs still tend to focus on qualifications and work history, some of which may be very relevant for some roles but, as we have seen, really depend more on the opportunities a candidate has been able to access rather than their real qualities and potential.

Shortlisting questions:

As we have seen, most of the information found on traditional CVs is not relevant to the role, and may well put recruiters off for no good reason. If we could replace the irrelevant stuff with relevant and useful information, how much better would the process be for everyone involved?

So, for example, in advance of advertising, the hiring managers agree the top, say, four or five strengths that a candidate absolutely must have in order to be able to carry out the role effectively. In some cases, this may justifiably include specific work experience or qualifications, which can be included if they are absolutely vital to the role.
Then questions are devised relating specifically to each of

those strengths. Candidates are invited to apply not with CVs and cover letters, but with answers to these questions. The (anonymised) answers are then given to the shortlisting panel.

There are two huge advantages to this method. The first is that prospective candidates will have a much better idea of what the role really requires, and it's more likely that only suitable candidates will apply, saving time sifting through loads of CVs from patently unsuitable candidates.

The second – and awesome – advantage is that the only criteria used to shortlist candidates is around their suitability for the job. This is the only information the panel have access to, and provided the questions are well-designed and relevant, removes the potential for most biases.

Alternatives to interviews

Microsoft are keen to identify the best possible talent. Jenny Lay-Flurrie, their Chief Accessibility Officer, describes[4] why they changed their assessment processes: 'In the case of people with autism, the knowledge base and technical aptitude of individuals can be very high, so we had to figure out why we weren't placing them.

We discovered the problem—the interview process. We changed our approach to what the process should look like. Now we work with a local group to bring candidates in for a week-long academy. We offer team work and technical exercises, and a lot of training. At the end of the week, we have an idea of those who will receive a job offer.'

As a former amateur musician, I was interested in hearing about blind auditions for orchestras. Brown (2016)[2] tells the story better than I could:

'Consider the famous example of blind auditions: as late as 1970, the top five orchestras in the US had fewer than 5 per cent of women musicians. It wasn't until 1980 that any of these top orchestras had an increased representation at 10 per cent. But by 1977, they were up to 25 per cent, and today some of them have more than 30 per cent. Although the original impetus for blind auditions was, anecdotally, to root out biases for and against students of certain well-known teachers, the results of installing a curtain, laying down carpet to avoid the hearing of footsteps, and anonymising details from resumes also led to a dramatic rise in the number of female players accepted into major orchestras.'

In this example, musicians were assessed solely on their playing ability, with absolutely nothing else being taken into consideration. It isn't always possible to replicate that assessment method into all roles, but it's an approach which can and should be adapted as far as is practicable.
HS2, for example, have replaced CVs for some of their technical roles with blind online tests relevant to the job with no names attached. As a result, there has been a huge uptake in successful applications from women, candidates from ethnic minorities and disabled candidates.

Case Study: Evenbreak

We advise employers to make their recruitment processes as accessible as possible, but do we practice what we preach? Here is the process we used at Evenbreak in a recent hiring round, looking to fill two roles.

As a small social enterprise aimed at improving disability inclusion in the workplace, we have a policy of only employing disabled people ourselves. Our recruitment process therefore needs to be specifically developed to be both accessible and inclusive. However, we are also keen that our team is diverse in a much broader sense – diversity in terms of type of impairment, age, gender, ethnicity, sexual orientation, culture, thinking styles, educational background, location and so on.

We advertise vacancies on our own job board, which is promoted in various ways to disabled people (partnerships with universities, colleges, charities, welfare-to-work providers, Jobcentre Plus, disability journals, social media, online and offline forums, etc).

We offer decent salaries and holiday entitlements and development opportunities as well as flexible working to ensure we attract the best candidates.

The adverts describe our mission and values, an overview of the role, and how we will support the candidate (smart-working, flexibility, relevant adjustments etc). We focus on strengths rather than competences, making it clear that qualifications and experience aren't as important as drive, motivation and values, and that any protected characteristics (as defined in the Equality Act 2010) are irrelevant – our only interest is in what they can bring to the role.

Our approach is to state in the advert that we are not interested in which university the candidate went to, or what degree they got, or even whether they went to university at all. Neither are we particularly interested in their work history. What we are really interested in is what strengths they would bring to the role. The core strengths needed for the role in question are accurately described.

We make it clear that these may be strengths they were born with, or have developed – in or out of a work situation. And that they can demonstrate those strengths to us in ways which work best for them.

Every candidate who meets the minimum criteria is sent a job description and put through to the next stage automatically (this applies to disabled candidates, but as we only employ disabled people it applies to all candidates who identify as disabled and meet the minimum requirements).

The rest of the process – the assessment of each candidate's suitability for the role – is conducted on their terms. We state that we want them to have the best opportunity to shine in the assessment stage, and that we know the usual CV and interview process doesn't work for everyone. Candidates can demonstrate their strengths in any way which works for them – for example, written submission, video, conversation (face-to-face, telephone, Skype or email/messenger), examples of previous work etc.

Candidates can contact us (through telephone or email or whatever medium is accessible to them) to ask any questions they may have about the selection process, the company, or the role itself.

At each stage in the process candidates are asked if they would like any adjustments. As they know all the other candidates are also disabled, it is easier to request adjustments without worrying that this may disadvantage them.

Each candidate then engages in their chosen way to demonstrate they have the strengths we are looking for. The hiring decision is based purely on which candidate shows the most potential to add value to the business.
Each candidate (successful or otherwise) is offered comprehensive feedback and further advice if requested.

The outcomes of the process were that we had 41 applications – any one of whom would have been ideal. Written submissions were sent, telephone conversations had, face-to-face meetings took place, videos were watched, links were followed. Every candidate had the strengths we were looking for. What a great problem to have! We were spoilt for choice.

In the end, we appointed three candidates rather than two,

as we couldn't choose between two for one role, and then reluctantly rejected the remaining 38 candidates. The three candidates we appointed have turned out to be the most amazing people, both individually and as a team.

Feedback from unsuccessful candidates was that they found the process open and inviting, and even though they hadn't got the job, many had increased their confidence during the process and found the feedback we gave them useful.

The process resulted in attracting a diverse group of ideal candidates, three amazing new employees, and 38 great advocates for Evenbreak, some of whom we can hopefully employ in the future.

Work-based Tasks

Amir, mentioned earlier, asks, if you are assessing his coding skills, is it better to ask him in an interview how good he is at coding, or give him some to do, so he can show you? The answer should be obvious. You want to appoint the person who is best at coding, not the person who is best at talking about being the best at coding!

The same principle applies to many (most?) skills. If you need a chef, do you ask them how good they are at cooking, or give them some ingredients and ask them to prepare you a meal? If you are looking for a customer service representative, do you interview them, or give them a role play in dealing with a customer complaint?

Pacelli (2014)[20] agrees. He says, 'An autistic person can often most effectively show his skills through a sample activity, such as proofing a sample document for an editing position.' So does Booth[12] who suggests, 'Practical tests will usually provide a fairer means of assessing an autistic applicant.'

And of course, this doesn't just apply to autistic candidates. It applies to all candidates, and many roles. Having evidence of someone using a skill is far more reliable than hearing them talk about it.

There are some skills which can't easily be demonstrated in a practical way, of course. But scenario-based activities can often usefully supplement an interview. PwC's assessment centres, for example, are set up to represent a 'day at PwC' where the candidates are given realistic scenarios to work on as a team.

Virtual reality tests are increasingly being introduced to the recruitment process. These can test various skills of the candidate in a safe environment, but will tend to be unsuitable for most candidates with sight impairment.

Case study – Lloyds Banking Group[16]

Lloyds Banking Group gets thousands of applications for its Emerging Leadership Programme every year. To narrow the pool, it asks candidates to complete strengths and analytical tests followed by a video interview. But here's where it gets really interesting. The hundreds of candidates who reach the final round are evaluated in virtual reality as part of a day-long assessment centre visit. Using a virtual reality platform, candidates freely move within a 360-degree virtual world and manipulate objects using tracked motion controls. An evaluator judges how they approach and solve tasks, using standardised metrics to assess the strengths that Lloyds Banking Group is looking for.

This gives recruiters better ability to assess skills; instead of candidates describing how they would do a task, they actually do the task, giving Lloyds a first-hand look at behaviour. Also, there is less opportunity for unconscious bias. Evaluators are 'blind' to past experience. Diverse candidates across gender and BAME and disability exceed industry norms as a result. 96% of candidates rated the virtual reality experience as both comfortable and impressive, and 100% think it adds value to the hiring process.

Group interviews/tasks

For some roles, group tasks may work well, although we need to take account of particular access needs, such as autistic candidates not necessarily being comfortable in group situations, or Deaf candidates needing sign language support.

Frost & Kalman (2016)[1] suggest, 'We should hire in groups as opposed to a 1 to 1 basis, to reduce unconscious bias. Following the usual 1 to 1 style there is every likelihood that the candidates will be partly judged on dud criteria, like attractiveness. And on a 1 to 1 basis we select candidates individually, unaware of the bigger picture that we keep recruiting similar people. But if they are interviewed at the same time then the evaluation is more likely to be based on their skills and performance – and even if the interviewers are highly sceptical of the business case for diversity, they are still unlikely to put through five of the same people.'

They add, 'if you are observing 10 people at an assessment centre and you have to select five, the five are more likely to be diverse than if you interviewed 10 people 1 to 1.'

Written Tests

If the role requires good writing skills, then written tests may be appropriate. Ensure candidates are given any assistive technology they may require such as speech-to-text technology, or any other adjustments. Some may be able to use their own laptops or other technology. For autistic candidates, Booth (2016)[12] suggests that:

'Written assessments can be made more accessible to autistic applicants, with:

- a separate room to sit the tests, with low sensory stimuli
- extra time to complete the test
- questions in straightforward language
- graphic rather than text-only questions'

Online tests

If the role requires online skills, there's no reason why you shouldn't use online tests (either in the test centre, or remotely from the candidate's home).

As with all assessment methods though, adjustments should be offered. In a legal case reported by ITV[21] a disabled job applicant was found to have been discriminated against by BT, when the Court of Appeal decided, 'the reasonable adjustments [he requested] were not impractical; would not have disrupted BT's activities and did not put a strain on BT's resources.'

Dr Michael Wardlow, from the Equality Commission stated following this case that, 'All employers must recognise that they have a legal duty to be proactive and consider what reasonable adjustments would be appropriate.'

Psychometric/ Personality Tests

Booth[12] makes her views clear on this. She states, 'Stress interviews and psychometric/personality tests are inaccurate at best, abusive and discriminatory at worst. There is no place for them in a fair recruitment process.'

Many traditionally-used psychometric and personality tests have been shown to be biased, however can sometimes add to the mix of assessment methods.

Case Study – Citi[16]

Like many Wall Street firms, Citi used to recruit students from elite schools. But the company had no standard with which it could compare all applicants, and the narrow focus on schools was cutting it off from other rich sources of talent. So they piloted a survey that measures key soft skills. The tool creates a profile based on top-performing Citi employees against which candidates are compared. It also ranks candidates' soft skills strengths and weaknesses which allows Citi to conduct more informed interviews.

The impact of this resulted in a better assessment of soft skills. Citi now gets a much more holistic view of candidates rather than the previously narrow look at their technical skills. And crucially, they are achieving more talent pool diversity, as the tool is reducing 'tunnel vision' and helping Citi reach top candidates at historically untargeted schools.

Additionally, it resulted in a more positive candidate experience. All candidates receive immediate and personalised feedback on their top skill. Nearly 90% rate the experience positively.

Work Trials

From the recruiter's perspective, the most reliable way of predicting a candidate's ability to perform in a role, is to see them working in it. Whilst not practical for all roles, it is becoming increasingly popular for some roles in sectors such as hospitality, for candidates to have a week's work trial. The candidate is given basic training (for example, serving breakfast in a hotel), and then is supervised actually carrying out the role.

This gives the recruiter a really good idea about how the candidate will perform in that role, and it gives the candidate a realistic taster of the job, so they can decide if it is for them.

As a method, this works well for candidates with learning disabilities, who may not shine in an interview situation, but with the right training and support, will be able to demonstrate their abilities.

Supported Internships

These take the idea of work trials to a whole new level.

Supported internships are study programmes for those young people furthest away from the labour market, often with learning disabilities or complex needs. They take place on an employer's premises, supported with tutoring and by a range of partnerships.

The National Development Team for Inclusion recently conducted a survey that revealed over 1,000 young people have completed a supported internship, with 50 per cent moving into paid employment straight away.[22]

Huw Davies, CEO of the British Association for Supported Employment insists[22] a well-run internship can massively improve the lives of those with learning disabilities. He said, 'It's life-changing because the chances are if they don't get a job by the time they are 25, they are going to find very little chance of getting a job for the rest of their lives. So, it's life-changing to get them moving straight from education into employment — not just for them, but for their families.'

My introduction to the concept of supported internships was through a trial run at National Grid.

Case study – National Grid

A number of young people with complex needs from a local specialist college were taken on 5 days a week during term-time for a year, with an accompanying job coach. Some in an office setting, others in functions such as catering, reception or facilities.

My impression was that initially this was seen by staff as a good, if slightly trepidatious, thing to do. It would be giving disadvantaged young people an opportunity to learn, and gain experience, in a real work setting. Nothing wrong with that. But in the event, the overwhelming message I got from staff was about how much they and the organisation itself had gained from the project.

It was a true win/win situation. The employment rate for young people with learning disabilities is traditionally a woeful 6 – 7%. Following this programme, 60% of the students found paid work, with others going on to mainstream college and other training schemes. A truly impressive result!

The staff at National Grid who were involved with the programme were incredibly enthusiastic about the experience. They had learned how to feel comfortable and confident working with disabled people, they felt more positive about their employer, and they had closer links with the wider community.

I remember talking to one of the interns at the end of the first programme. A young man with learning disabilities and autism, he had a job in the post room at National Grid's head offices in Warwick. I asked him what he enjoyed about his work, and he confidently explained that he delivers the mail to people in different offices, and that he loves the welcome he gets when he enters each office. People smile, say hello and have a chat.

Following my conversation with him I challenged the job coach who was showing me round, as this young man seemed very confident and sociable for someone deemed to have complex needs. I was reassured that 12 months previously, he had not been able to maintain eye contact with anyone, spoke very few words, and mostly looked at the floor. The staff had watched him grow in confidence over the year, so that now he could converse confidently with a total stranger.

A fabulous outcome for him, and also the people around him.

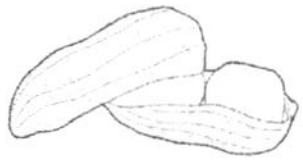

In a Nutshell:

Don't rely solely on CVs and interviews to assess the potential of your candidates – more effective ways are available

"Prejudice is a burden that confuses the past, threatens the future and renders the present inaccessible"

Maya Angelou, Author

Part Four:

Selection

Great Way #11: Unbiased Decision-Making

No matter how inclusive your recruitment strategies are up to this point, it will all have been for nothing if the final hiring decision is biased.

Most organisations now have a panel of people making the final decision, rather than leaving it to one person, which can iron out at least some of the potential biases. The danger, however, with a group of people is the phenomenon of 'group think'. There are a couple of ways to mitigate against this.

The first one is to have a diverse range of people on the panel. This could mean diversity in terms of ethnicity, gender, age, seniority and so on, and also by including people with lived experience of disability.

The second is for each member of the panel to individually score each shortlisted candidate against the criteria agreed at the beginning of the process, before coming together to compare notes. Otherwise, there is a danger that everyone will agree with the most senior person in the room, or the one with the loudest voice.

Tarki (2019)[24] says that, 'Most senior executives I've worked with have believed they are mature enough to listen to everyone and not be negatively influenced by each other. I don't doubt their sincerity in this. I have, however, not seen any evidence suggesting that executives are immune to being influenced by a group.'

To give everyone an equal voice, interviewers shouldn't share candidate feedback until they meet as a group, they should give interviewees a numerical score and they should write down their take on candidates first, so they can come prepared to offer their perspective.

Training of people given the responsibility to make hiring decisions is important. There has been much focus in recent years of training in unconscious bias, and there are varying views on its effectiveness.

The fact that unconscious (and conscious) bias can and will skew decision-making against certain groups is almost universally accepted.

Kalman and Frost (2016)[1] state that, 'Unconscious bias is omnipresent in organisations and likely to be more prevalent at times of stress and change (or when recruitment is done in a hurry)'. As recruitment is often both stressful and done in a hurry, unconscious bias is likely to be a factor in hiring decisions.

Banaji and Greenwald (2016)[25] suggest that, 'Hidden biases are capable of guiding our behaviour without our being aware of their role.' This may seem difficult to believe, and they go on to say, 'Most people find it unbelievable that their behaviour can be guided by mental content of which they are unaware.'

In recruitment circles, we talk about the "horns" and "halo" effects. If we like a candidate (maybe because they are similar to us, or similar to the previous role-holder) we tend to look only for positive traits, and ignore the less positive, creating a "halo" effect.

Conversely, if we don't like a candidate (maybe they are different from what we expected, or don't immediately conform to our ideal image of the perfect candidate) we are likely to be actively looking for reasons to justify our negative first impression, and will ignore the positive traits of that candidate – the "horns" effect.

Proponents of training in unconscious bias believe that it can be effective in mitigating its effects. Brown (2016)[2] suggests, 'If we can all better understand how unconscious bias works and cultivate awareness of our individual biases, then we can avoid limiting or damaging our ability to lead, to make decisions, and to be better colleagues.'

She goes on to say, 'We may inevitably perceive the world through our own lenses, but we can also challenge our perception that everyone else is working with the same understanding and perspective. If we work to cultivate a better understanding of how others experience the same environments and situations, we'll raise our own intuition about our interactions. That intuition is essential to building workplaces and market spaces that are more welcoming, more comfortable, and more inclusive.'

Surely, identifying our unconscious bias and making it conscious, we can consciously eliminate it? Apparently not. Banaji and Greenwald (2016)[25] developed the IAT (Implicit Association Test), which identifies bias towards or against various groups of people. In taking the tests themselves, in common with most people, they identified their own unconscious bias. Unfortunately, the results of the test barely changed over time as they took them repeatedly. Awareness of the hidden bias did not seem to help to eradicate them.

In some cases, the concept of unconscious bias can be counter-productive. We can't be expected to bear responsibility for actions governed by biases we are unaware of. Discriminatory behaviour can almost be excused, because it was done unconsciously.

Instead of focusing on unconscious bias, perhaps instead we should be promoting conscious inclusion. Finding ways to eliminate, or at least reduce, the opportunity for bias – unconscious or otherwise – would be more productive.

One method is to use strategies such as blind CVs and interviews, or more effective alternatives to both, as described previously.

Regular training in disability awareness and inclusive

recruitment strategies should be delivered to everyone involved in the recruitment process.

Eliminating group think using the methods described earlier in this chapter is also important.

A strategy described by Banaji and Greenwald (2016)[25] is to 'develop evidence-based guidelines to eliminate discretion from judgments that might otherwise afford opportunity for hidden-bias mindbugs to operate. When faithfully applied, intelligently developed guidelines will leave little room for hidden biases.' Which takes us back to setting objective criteria, discussed much earlier in this book.

Common perceptions of disabled people are generally negative (benefit scroungers, workshy, 'less good' etc), and even the positive stereotypes (e.g. Paralympians) are not seen as relevant to recruiters or employers. Positive images of disabled people in mainstream media, particularly in relation to employment, are far too rare.

Much work needs to be done in changing the narrative around disabled people so that we are seen as valuable members of society with a positive contribution to make.

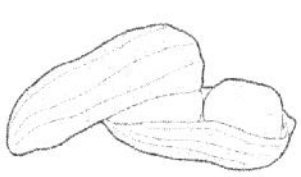

In a nutshell:
Make sure the hiring decision is made by a group of people trained in inclusive recruitment, using objective criteria

"If we don't pro-actively and consciously include, we will unconsciously exclude"

Stephen Frost

Great Way #12: Job Offer and Induction

The recruitment process doesn't end with the hiring decision – the job offer has to made (and accepted), unsuccessful candidates need to be informed, and the successful candidate(s) need to be inducted/onboarded.

Job Offer

This is pretty straightforward, but just a note to make sure you don't fail at the final hurdle! Make sure the job offer is accessible.

One company did everything brilliantly throughout the recruitment process, ensuring that barriers were removed, and adjustments provided. The candidate who shone as by far the best, happened to be blind.

The company sent him his offer letter through the post, accompanied by a (hard copy) catalogue of assistive technology to browse through. Unfortunately, the candidate turned the job down because he had been sent inaccessible information – a regrettable mistake by the company – and they lost their best candidate.

Unsuccessful candidates

A common complaint from candidates, disabled and non-disabled alike, is the lack of feedback from recruiters.

Using some of the methods described in this book, you

should drastically reduce the number of unsuitable applications you receive. Hopefully, this will mean avoiding having hundreds of CVs to sift through from people clearly not suitable for the role. With fewer, but better quality, applicants, giving feedback is not so time-consuming.

It is unrealistic to be expected to offer personalised, high quality feedback on every application you receive, but an acknowledgement of receipt and a short, polite rejection for those not short-listed is not unreasonable (and I know many recruiters who fail to provide this minimum courtesy).

For candidates who have been put forward to the next stage, it should be standard practice to offer feedback to those who are unsuccessful, as the numbers will be much lower.

Onboarding/induction

Having recruited your best candidate(s), it's important for them to start their career with you on the right footing. In addition to the onboarding process offered to all new recruits, you will need to have a conversation around any workplace adjustments required in order to reduce or remove the barriers they might face.

The new recruit is likely to know what adjustments will work for them. It might be flexible working hours to avoid the rush hour commute. It might be some specialist software. It might be keeping the walkways clear to avoid a tripping hazard. Have a conversation about adjustments they have previously used in the workplace or at home.

It may be that you, and they, need support in identifying what options are available. You are not expected to be an expert in this – there are plenty of organisations out there who are. Access to Work is a government initiative which helps disabled people find, and pay for, the adjustments they need. They will send an assessor out to make recommendations.

Adjustments should be put in place as quickly as possible. I know of an intern whose assistive technology didn't arrive until the last day of his internship. Meaning he was unable to demonstrate his true skills throughout, and lost out on the opportunity of a permanent job.

Another new recruit with visual impairment required a large monitor. When it still failed to arrive months later, she'd had significant time off sick with the migraines that using an unsuitable monitor had caused. She failed her probation period (almost certainly illegally) through no fault of her own.

In a nutshell:
Recruitment is just the start of the process. It's important that the new recruit's experience is inclusive and welcoming

"Vision without action is merely a dream. Action without vision just passes the time. Vision with action can change the world"

Joel A. Barker

Bonus Way

Great Way #13: Guaranteed Shortlisting

This is usually known as a “Guaranteed Interview Scheme” (GIS). We have changed the title here, as increasingly employers are using more effective ways than interviews alone to assess candidates’ suitability for roles.

A GIS guarantees a disabled candidate an interview, or whatever the next stage in the recruitment process might be, **if** they meet the minimum criteria for the role (clearly interviewing someone who doesn’t meet the essential criteria would be a waste of their time and yours). It can be a good way of ensuring that talented candidates aren’t overlooked because of assumptions about their suitability due to their impairment which might affect their CV, work experience, or the perceptions of the recruiter. The candidate would still be assessed alongside others on merit, and only appointed if they are the best candidate, but it can ensure that the best candidate isn’t lost through perceptions rather than reality.

There are mixed views about these schemes. They are currently a requirement of the Disability Confident Scheme. Some recruiters worry that they will be inundated with unsuitable disabled candidates (we don’t think this has ever happened). Some disabled candidates see it is favouritism and would rather be assessed on their merits.

However, I believe it is good practice to offer this as an option. A disabled candidate can then choose whether to take advantage of it or not. A simple statement such as:

'If you identify as having a disability or long-term health condition, and meet all the essential criteria, we offer a guaranteed shortlisting to the next stage in the recruitment process. Please tick here if you qualify and would like to be included.'

Frost[10] wrote about recruiting people for the London Olympics. He says, 'Thousands of talented disabled people, understandably sceptical about employer platitudes, applied to work for LOCOG. The key element of the >access now programme, which convinced the sceptics more than anything else, was the guaranteed interview if they met the minimum criteria. This promise was enough to convince talented disabled people to spend the time and effort applying to us as they could guarantee that all-important first foot in the door.'

Offering guaranteed shortlisting for disabled candidates who meet the minimum criteria gives a powerful message that you are serious about hiring disabled people.

Frost & Kalman[1] suggest that, 'One of the most effective ways to circumvent cynicism and connect with untapped talent is to demonstrate intent through guaranteeing interviews to qualified disabled people.'

Offer the option for guaranteed shortlisting for anyone who

identifies as having a disability or long-term health condition (including the latter term as many people don't necessarily identify as being disabled, or still see it as a stigma), and who meet the essential criteria for the role. It's important to make it clear that the hiring decision will be merit-based.

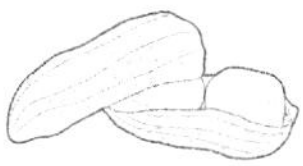

In a nutshell:

Offering disabled candidates who meet the minimum criteria optional guaranteed shortlisting demonstrates commitment to positive action

A Quick Word About Technology

The rapid advances of technology have created, in the main, huge opportunities for disabled candidates and those trying to attract them. Those opportunities have to be carefully examined, however, as they may exclude or disadvantage some candidates.

The ability to search for jobs and apply online has been available for many years now, and can be very helpful to people who find it difficult to get out and about. It can be much quicker and easier to carry out these tasks from home. It's important to remember, though, that not everyone has access to the internet, or owns a device, or understands how to use technology.

The ability for video interviewing can be helpful for candidates who have difficulty in travelling, or who find it less threatening to be in their own home (although see previous chapters about interviewing). Video can also be an effective way for some candidates to demonstrate their skills.

The rise in smart phones, and their inherent accessibility, has enabled many people to access job opportunities on their smart phones, and indeed, most candidates do use their phones to search for jobs now.

The more recent introduction of AI (Artificial Intelligence) into recruitment processes has been received with both excitement and trepidation.

Initially it was enthusiastically received by recruiters as it can offer a huge saving of time (in sifting CVs and conducting interviews). Time to hire, as mentioned previously, still being seen as important. It was also hailed as the magic bullet in eliminating bias in recruitment. A machine can't discriminate, surely?

HireVue, quoted by Leech (2019)[26], state, 'AI-driven approach mitigates bias by eliminating unreliable and inconsistent variables like selection based on resume and phone screens, allowing you to focus on more job-relevant criteria.'

However, Leech suggests, 'Artificial intelligence has been regularly in the news, not for solving bias but maintaining it. Several studies have found that AI perpetuates and bolsters bias.'

An example is a system Amazon develop to assess CVs. Amazon's computer models were trained to vet applicants by observing patterns in résumés submitted to the company over a 10-year period. Most came from men, a reflection of male dominance across the tech industry. In effect, Amazon's system taught itself that male candidates were preferable, downgrading candidates who mentioned the word 'women's' or who went to all female educational establishments.

Some AI applications, when interviewing, scans the face of the person speaking, picking up on cues which might be missed by a human recruiter. These cues include facial expressions and eye-contact which will gauge the interaction with the task. I'm sure you can see the dangers in this when it comes to candidates with a range of impairments.

Leech concludes, 'Both unconscious bias in face-to-face interviews and AI technology could and should be improved but, until machine learning has proven itself to be the far better option, the transition should be made tentatively.'

Polli (2019)[27] reminds us that 'The deepest-rooted source of bias in AI is the human behavior it is simulating. It is the biased data set used to train the algorithm. If you don't like what the AI is doing, you definitely won't like what humans are doing because AI is purely learning from humans.'

She suggests that the current way of assessing candidates is far from bias. In cases where there is a large number of applicants, they are often sifted quickly to reduce the number on unfair grounds – which university they went to, or having experience within a similar organisation. This doesn't lead to an increased diversity of candidates – in fact, it's likely to do the opposite.

The problem of bias, she maintains, can be successfully addressed by AI. She says, 'A beauty of AI is that we can design it to meet certain beneficial specifications. … One key principle is that AI should be designed so it can be audited and the bias found in it can be removed. An AI audit should function just like the safety testing of a new car before someone drives it. If standards are not met, the defective technology must be fixed before it is allowed into production.'

Noel Sharkey, a professor of AI and robotics at the University of Sheffield, suggested that AI decision-making should be tested in the same way as new pharmaceutical drugs are evaluated before they are released to the market.[28] He believes that, 'they should be tested on hundreds of thousands of people in order to eradicate major in-built biases in the data they use.'

Whatever its advantages and disadvantages, AI is clearly disrupting the recruitment sector. Peccarelli (2019)[29] suggests that increasingly recruiters will not only need to have the technical acumen to deal with today's challenges, but the flexibility to adapt to those of tomorrow.

He believes that, 'Ultimately, what the rise of AI is proving consistently is that the companies that will thrive in uncertain times are those with a relentless commitment to innovation, creativity, collaboration and learning, and with a diverse workforce that can anticipate trends and spot new threats from the least likely places.'

I think the message is that whilst AI isn't a magic button to eliminate bias, our traditional methods aren't any better. AI is a tool, and like any other tools, needs to be made fit for purpose, and thoroughly tested. I suspect there is huge potential for AI to add something really useful to the recruitment process, but there will always be the need for a human touch.

And Finally ...

Of all the suggestions in this book, this one pretty much covers everything. We've talked about the social model previously. There is nothing 'wrong' with a disabled candidate or employee. What needs changing isn't the candidate, it's the barriers we (recruiters, employers, and more broadly, society) put in the way. If we remove the barriers, those candidates will still have impairments, but they will be much less disabled.

If I could sum up this book in one sentence, it would be "through identifying and removing the barriers disabled candidates face, your organisation will attract and retain unimaginable talent". Easy to say, I know.

Sweeney and Bothwick (2016)[6] suggest that:
'Regardless of how supportive and committed the senior team are, regardless of how passionate your employee networks are and regardless of how "bias blind" your organisation says they are, there will be barriers, obstacles and challenges to overcome through the life of creating the change.'

'Many companies now ask for diverse candidate slates, sometimes by setting a target, but still too often, the overarching policy at leadership level doesn't translate down to the activity of the hiring manager. The firm is saying how committed they are to receiving a diverse slate of candidates, but the manager just wants to fill the slot – ideally with someone similar to the person they are replacing.'

They identified the four main types of barriers as Structural, Procedural, Attitudinal and Skills and Knowledge.

Structural barriers could be physical, such as an inaccessible building (perhaps not wheelchair-accessible, or maybe too open-plan and noisy for someone with autism), or it could be about the management structure, and where/if diversity and inclusion sits within it. However, if your building isn't wheelchair-accessible (and sadly, most aren't), this certainly doesn't mean you can't employ disabled people. Around 5% of disabled people use wheelchairs, so there is still the other 95% - and those with mobility issues may well be able to work remotely.

Procedural barriers tend to be policy-based and could include inaccessible recruitment processes, or how people are selected for redundancy, or training, or development opportunities.

Attitudinal barriers are the most difficult to remove. If hiring managers genuinely believe that disabled people are a hindrance, the best recruitment process in the world won't be fair.

Lack of appropriate skills and knowledge is easier to manage, but still very common. Wanting to achieve something and knowing how to are two different things. Make sure you are tackling the root cause of the barrier not just the symptom (e.g. if you have a low number of disabled people applying for jobs, find out why – it may not just be that you're not advertising in the right places, it might be that your organisation has a poor reputation of offering appropriate and timely support to disabled employees)

When we talk to employers about employing disabled people, one of the questions we are often asked is what you should put in place first.

In some ways, that's an odd question, because you are almost certainly already employing disabled people. You just might not know. Most impairments (around 80%) are not visible, so many people just don't mention them. Consider dyslexia, diabetes, asthma, chronic pain, autism, mental health conditions and so on.

Apart from that, if we waited for organisations to become completely inclusive before employing disabled people, no disabled person would ever be employed! The important starting point is to just get started. It's a virtuous circle – the more disabled people you employ, the easier it gets, and the more confident you become.

On the whole, disabled candidates understand that no organisation will get everything right every time, but if there is a willingness to listen and learn that's enough.
Disability inclusion is, of course, at the heart of everything we do at Evenbreak, and we are still learning. We are incredibly lucky because we have loads of opportunities to learn – from our amazing candidates, our enthusiastic employers, and each other. Within the Evenbreak team, we

have a wide array of impairments and learn something new from each other all the time.

The danger is that if you wait until everyone is trained, all the buildings are made accessible, all the policies are changed and all the budgets are in place, it will never happen. You can still be working on all of those things in parallel with attracting disabled people to help you on that journey.

Sometimes the 'we can't do it until …' becomes an excuse rather than a genuine concern. In particular, budgets! If this is really a priority for you, you'll find the budget from somewhere.

So – what's ***really*** stopping you?

Sources

1. Frost, F. & Kalman, D. *Inclusive Talent Management.* Kogan Page, 2016

2. Brown, J. *Inclusion: Diversity, the new workplace and the will to change.* Purpose Driven Publishing, 2016

3. Hatton, J. *A Dozen Brilliant Reasons to Employ Disabled People.* Elite Publishing Academy, 2017

4. Kennedy, T. *Getting to Equal 2018: The Disability Inclusion Advantage.* Accenture Research, 2018

5. Tsusaki, M. et al. *The Business Imperative of Diversity.* Boston Consulting Group, 2019

6. Sweeney, C. & Bothwick, F. *Inclusive Leadership.* Pearson, 2016

7. von Schrader, S. et al. *Emerging Employment Issues for People with Disabilities.* Cornell University, 2010

8. *Job Board Report 2019.* Applied. www.beapplied.com. 2019

9. Patel, J. & Yafai, G. *Demystifying Diversity.* Gilgamesh Publishing Ltd., 2016

10. Frost, Stephen. *The Inclusion Imperative.* Kogan Page,

2014

11. *Barriers to Employment*. Evenbreak and Enactus, 2020

12. Booth, J. *Autism Equality in the Workplace*. Jessica Kingsley Publishing, 2016

13. *Six ways to make the most of your job ads*. Reed (www.reed.co.uk)

14. *What Workers Want Report 2018*. Hays, 2018

15. Schmidt, J. et al. *Does Emphasizing Different Types of Person–Environment Fit in Online Job Ads Influence Application Behavior and Applicant Quality? Evidence from a Field Experiment*. Journal of Business and Psychology. (pp 267–282) June, 2015

16. LinkedIn Talent Solutions. *Reinventing the Interview*. Global Recruiting Trends, 2018

17. Nisbett, R. *Why Job Interviews are Pointless*. The Guardian, 22 November, 2015

18. Dana, J. et al. *Belief in the unstructured interview: The persistence of an illusion*. Judgment and Decision Making, Vol. 8, No. 5 (pp. 512–520), 2013

19. Dana, J. *The Utter Uselessness of Job Interviews*. The New York Times, 8 April, 2017

20. Pacelli, P. *Six Word Lessons for Autism Friendly Workplaces*. Washington: Pacelli Publishing, 2014

21. *Court of Appeal upholds discrimination case against BT*. ITV Report, 31 July 2019

22.Jordan, L. *Supported internships are a success story for young people with SEND*. FE Week, 10 March 2019

23. Devine, D. *Do supported internships deliver the jobs and improved life chances that they promise?* Learning Disability Today, 31 May 2019

24. Tarki, A. *How to Avoid Groupthink When Hiring*. Harvard Business Review, 13 August 2019

25. Banaji, M. & Greenwald, A. *Blindspot*. Bantam Books, 2016

26. Leech, E. *The Perils of AI Recruitment*. New Statesman Tech, 14 August 2019

27. Polli, F. *Using AI to Eliminate Bias from Hiring*. Harvard Business Review, 29 October 2019

28. Webber, A. *Recruitment algorithms are 'infected with biases', AI expert warns*. Personnel Today, 13 December 2019

29. Peccarelli, B. *AI isn't taking our jobs - but it is changing how we recruit*. World Economic Forum, 14 January 2019

Further Reading

There are new articles and books being written on this exciting topic all the time, and my advice would be to keep reading and learning to keep on top of advances in this field. In addition to the sources quoted in this book, some of my current favourites include:

Mildon, T. *Inclusive Growth*. Rethink Press, 2020

Companies often struggle to know how to integrate inclusion, and in this book, Toby offers a practical framework to design and implement a sustainable inclusivity infrastructure, from gaining clarity right through to celebration.

Ruh, D. *Tapping Into Hidden Human Capital*. G3ict, 2016

This book takes a global perspective, examining how leading global companies have improved their bottom line by employing disabled people. It looks at global trends, and different approaches taken in different countries.

Nielsen, T. & Kepinski, L. Inclusion Nudges. www.inclusion-nudges.org, 2016

This amazing book is packed full of simple and practical techniques for changing behaviour, culture and systems to create inclusive organisations. Great for prompting interesting conversations about the everyday impact of inclusion (or lack of it).

Swain, J. et al (eds). *Disabling Barriers – Enabling Environments.* Sage, 2004

Although it's been around for a while, the essays in this book, written by greats such as Mike Oliver, Vic Finkelstein and Liz Carr, offer much modern-day wisdom.

Acknowledgements

I am eternally grateful for knowing so many people who are generous enough to share their learnings and experiences with me, and who have helped me grow as a person.

Those I have learned the most from are the strong women in my family. My late mother was a remarkable woman, who was way ahead of her time and taught me so much about equality, and the importance of promoting independence for everyone. Independence of decision-making, as well as physical independence. At the end of her life, severely disabled and requiring much support, her choice was to remain at home rather than move into a care home. I'm proud that we were able to respect this decision, difficult though it was at times.

Her strength lives on in my wonderful daughters. Alexandra's vocation from the age of 10 was to be a teacher, and from about 13 was to teach children with additional needs. Now she heads up a base for children with autism, and I couldn't be more proud of her.

Philippa's passion is international development. She has worked with street children in Africa, rural communities in India, refugees in Greece and is currently in Australia. I have vicariously learned from her experiences, and am equally proud of her.

I learn from both of them all the time, and now another

strong woman has joined the family – my granddaughter Talia! Still a toddler (and already showing traits of knowing her own mind), she motivates me to do all I can to ensure the world she grows up in is inclusive, and values everyone.

Outside of my family, I am also fortunate to be surrounded by amazing people. The team at Evenbreak has a wealth of lived experience, and we learn from each other all the time. Enabling everyone to use their very diverse and immense strengths requires finding new ways of working – both in terms of flexibility and the use of technology. We are always learning and improving how we work, and can pass this learning onto others.

Our candidates are a constant source of new ideas. The research carried out for us (referenced in the book) engaged with over 700 disabled people, who were so generous with their time, and so honest and open with their experiences. Feedback from them informs our understanding and our practice.

Some of the employers we work with are pioneering new ideas (whose case studies I was able to include in the book), and they are open to sharing both their challenges and their successes with others. I welcome this generosity, meaning we can all benefit.

Evenbreak doesn't work in isolation, and we work with many partners (particularly those led by disabled people) to raise awareness and support employers to become more inclusive and accessible. Every organisation has something unique to offer, and again, I learn so much from working with people with a range of lived experiences.

And I am very grateful to those who took the time to read the book before being published, in particular, Michael Vermeersch, Graeme Whippy and Simon Clements for offering their insights to inform some great improvements.

Finally, huge thanks to you, for reading the book, and for having an interest in creating a more inclusive and accessible workplace for everyone. I hope you were able to take something from it that you can implement in practice. If so, I'd love to hear about it – do let me know!

Printed in Great Britain
by Amazon

71709500R00098